Fire in the Deep

Fire in the Deep

Lectio Divina Series
Cycle A

Robert J. Miller

SHEED & WARD

Franklin, Wisconsin
Chicago

As an apostolate of the Priests of the Sacred Heart, a Catholic religious congregation, the mission of Sheed & Ward is to publish books of contemporary impact and enduring merit in Catholic Christian thought and action. The books published, however, reflect the opinion of their authors and are not meant to represent the official position of the Priests of the Sacred Heart.

2001

Sheed & Ward
7373 South Lovers Lane Road
Franklin, Wisconsin 53132
1-800-266-5564

Scripture quotations are lectionary based.

Printed in the United States of America

Cover and interior design: GrafixStudio, Inc.

Library of Congress Cataloging-in-Publication Data

Miller, Robert J., priest.
    Fire in the deep : lecto divina series, cycle A / Robert J. Miller.
      p.cm.
   ISBN 1-58051-107-4 (pbk.)
   Devotional calendars—Catholic Church. 2. Bible—Meditations.
     3. Catholic Church—Prayer-books and devotions—English.
     4. Catholic Church. Lectionary for Mass (U.S.) Year A I. Title.

BX2182.3 .M55 2001
242'.3—dc21   2001042997

1 2 3 4 5 / 04 03 02 01

Dedication

To all those past and present people in my life
who helped light the Fire within,
who kept the Fire burning through twenty-five years,
who taught me the importance of being on Fire in the first place.

In this Jubilee Year of my priesthood,
a special recognition to these "Fire-starters":

June Marnell
Bert and Ollie Finn
Fr. Marv Mottet
Therese Gaffney
Kathy Reznicek
Fr. Louie Miller
Steve Hrycyniak
Fr. John Harvey
Joe and Marsha Menke

And my parents "in glory,"
Bob and Stell Miller

FOREWORD

The first president Bush asked an elderly nursing home resident, "Do you know who I am?" "No," goes the apocryphal reply, "but if you ask one of the nurses, she can tell you."

It's important to know who we are. The problem is, we don't always know where to go to find out. President Bush was lucky; somebody told him. But as people of faith, as people of the Book, we, too, are lucky, for we have a place to go that tells us very clearly who we are. And that place is the Word of God.

Many people make the mistake of thinking we read Scripture to find out *what to do*. But first and foremost, Scripture seeks to tell us *who we are*. And this is what it says: we are beloved children of a loving God who made us good and gave us a destiny that is eternal life. The late liturgist Rev. Eugene Walsh, S.S., used to say, "Jesus promises you only two things: your life has meaning and you're going to live forever." Then he would add, "If you get a better offer, take it!"

We're not going to get a better offer because there's nothing better than knowing we belong to God and knowing Christ made possible an eternity of dwelling in God's love. Author Stanley Hauerwas says the value of knowing who we are is that it helps us figure out what to do. Our *identity* sets our agenda, he says, not a legal code, a list of dos and don'ts imposed from the outside. We start with who we are—then we figure out what to do.

Some teenagers (and not a few adults, unfortunately) think Scripture was written to spoil their fun. All they see are lists of dos and don'ts. But they're coming at things backwards. They don't realize that Scripture is simply a description of what it looks like to live like who we say we are. Scripture tells us not only that we're beloved children of a loving God but also what such children look like: they're honest, faithful, compassionate, etc.

Knowing that, we ask ourselves: What do honest people do? They don't tell lies. What do compassionate people do? They care for each other and don't take advantage of the weak.

A recent scientific study examined the brain functioning of subjects as they looked at photos of people they loved. The conclusion was that contemplating the face of the one you love actually turns off those parts of the brain responsible for thinking and for depression. The media stressed that the study supported the long-held belief that "falling in love" seems to shut down some of our critical thinking processes. Love is blind after all, they announced! But there is a greater truth implied here: by releasing endorphins that promote bliss and turn off the parts of the brain that lead to weary, heavy hearts, focusing on the one we love also keeps us from lapsing into depression and despair.

The saints of our tradition understood that. Who are saints but people who know who they are and who know the Lord as their Beloved? How do they acquire such intimate knowledge of Christ? Usually, they do it through prayer, reading of Scripture, and seeking Christ in the face of their neighbor. They know him because they spend time with him—in prayer, in the Word, in others. They spend time with him because they know we have to spend time with someone in order to fall in love. And when we spend time with someone, that person rubs off on us. That person changes us in some way. Saints don't need scientific studies to teach them that contemplating the face of their Beloved transforms their lives. Intuition and grace are enough for them.

What the saints do, we can do. In fact, we must do it if we want to retain the identity we were given at baptism. And that's where a book like this comes in. Father Bob Miller has created a doorway into the Scripture of the lectionary. He invites us in not just to read, but to live in the Word. He invites us to spend time with our Beloved. His reflections are valuable most especially for the reflection they elicit *from* us.

His stories work because they draw our own stories out of us. More than anything, a book like this gives us space, sacred space, within which to engage important life questions: Who am I? Why am I here? Where am I going?

Father Bob helps us see why and how God's Word is our best companion on the road to discovering and becoming who we are meant to be. His love for the Word calls forth our own. His knowledge of Christ deepens ours. The more we read, the more convinced we become that the Christian life cannot be lived apart from God's Word. The more we read the more we understand the truth of St. Jerome's axiom: "Ignorance of Scripture is ignorance of Christ."

How important is all of this? It makes the difference between life and death, between being an *imago Dei*, an "image of God," and becoming *curvatus in se*, that is, "turned-in on the self," twisted and distorted by sin to the point that our likeness to God is nearly obliterated. A wonderful story illustrates this truth and underscores the absolute necessity of remaining rooted in the Word if we want to put on Christ and be his presence in the world.

When Leonardo da Vinci set out to paint his masterpiece, *The Last Supper*, he sought a model to pose for his image of Christ. Looking for someone whose face reflected both an outer and inner beauty, he finally found a young man, a chorister in one of the churches of Rome, who truly was beautiful both in face and character. His name was Pietro Bandinelli. The young man sat for da Vinci and became the face of Jesus.

After some years, the painting remained unfinished. Although da Vinci had painted all the other disciples, one face eluded him—that of Judas, Christ's betrayer. Da Vinci searched about until one night, on the streets of Rome, he found a man whose face was so distorted by sin that even da Vinci shuddered to look at him. *I have found my Judas*, thought the artist. The man posed and, at last, the painting was finished. Just as he was about to dismiss his Judas, however, da Vinci realized he had not asked the man's name. The man looked up and said, "But we have met before. My name is Pietro Bandinelli. I also posed for your image of Christ.[1]

Life and death. *Imago* or *curvatus*. These are our choices. They make a difference. We have been given a great gift and the means to hold on to it.

May your time with this book and the Scripture it celebrates make your life a celebration of the One who made us to know him in our minds, in our hearts, and in every day and every action of our lives.

—Graz Marcheschi
Director, Lay Ministry Formation
Archdiocese of Chicago

1. Gerard Fuller, OMI, *Stories for All Seasons* (Mystic, CT: Twenty-Third Publications, 1995), p. 98.

"Fire in the Deep"

> "[A person] must go on a quest
> to discover the sacred fire
> in the sanctuary of his own belly,
> to ignite the flame in his heart,
> to fuel the blaze in the hearth . . ."
>
> Sam Keen
> (*Fire in the Belly*, Bantam Books, 1991)

> *Mount Sinai was all wrapped in smoke,*
> *for the Lord came down upon it in fire.*
>
> Exodus 19:18

In January 1989, after twenty years as a vowed religious, and thirteen as a priest, I took an indefinite leave of absence from full-time ministry. It was perhaps the most difficult and challenging period of my life, but a much needed "season" in my life journey. For the next year and a half, I wrestled with vital but difficult life issues and God issues. At the end of that period, much had clarified and solidified for me, but one immutable fact stood out most clearly above all the rest.

There was a "Fire" burning deep within me that would not be extinguished. That "Fire in the Deep" had burned a "divine wound" onto me that was both identity and ideal (cf. Genesis 32:25–32). It had become obvious who I was, to whom I belonged, and what I was called to do at that particular moment of Life. Long ago, another person had spoken accurately what I was feeling at that time.

> "I say to myself 'I will not speak of him,'
> > but then it becomes like a fire
> burning in my heart, imprisoned in my bones;
> > I grow weary holding it in,
> I cannot endure it" (Jeremiah 20:9).

Thus, I returned to the active practice of my priesthood in June 1990—rekindled in energy, refocused in direction, and recommitted to humble service of the Good News. That "Fire" of God's Spirit burning within me was a unrelenting whisper that could not be ignored. "Preaching the Gospel is not the subject of a boast; I am under compulsion and have no choice. I am ruined if I do not preach it" (1 Corinthians 9:16). Now, over a decade later, it is clear that I became a far better priest because of my leave—and a far better man because of the Passion of God unleashed within.

Six hundred years before Christ, another servant of God had the same experience. After years of frustrating ministry and rejection by his people, the prophet Jeremiah grew tired of his role, and complained to God. He cried out to God saying, "You have tricked me, Lord, and I let myself be tricked! I say to myself, 'I'll never speak of him again!'" (Jeremiah 20:7–9) But quickly Jeremiah realized that he could never escape God's transforming role and Fiery Presence. "You were too strong for me, and you triumphed! It becomes like fire burning in my heart . . ." (Jeremiah 9:7).

Both of us discovered an attribute of God overlooked by our materialistic world, an often superficial Church and a recently centralizing hierarchy. *Our God is truly like Fire.* The Fire at the heart of Deity is patently uncontrollable, radically transformative, and utterly irresistible. Indeed, Moses' earliest experience of this Deity at Sinai was as Fire: "The Lord came down upon it in fire" (Exodus 19:18). John the Baptist's description of his divine Savior-cousin was that "he would baptize you in the Holy Spirit and fire" (Matthew 3:11).

God's Love moving in the human spirit is like the flames of a fire searing the deepest landscapes of one's inner world. Once the Spirit of

Jesus begins moving within a person, there can truly be no turning back, and no resisting. God is a relentless "Hound of Heaven," forever chasing you, a fire burning up all that stands between you and full surrender, a passionate Lover pursuing and chasing and never taking "no" for an answer.

Scripture is full of references to this "Fire" that is our God, and the "fiery" impact God's words have on sincere and committed believers.

> "The angel touched my mouth with the ember . . . I heard God say, 'Who shall I send? Who will go for us?' 'Here I am,' I said, 'Send me'" (Isaiah 6:6–8).

> "The Ancient One took his throne . . . his throne was flames of fire, with wheels of burning fire. A surging stream of fire flowed out from where he sat; thousands upon thousands were ministering to him" (Daniel 7:9–10).

> "Who can stand when he appears? For he is like the refiner's fire" (Malachi 3:2).

> "He will baptize you in the Holy Spirit and fire" (Matthew 3:11).

It is this illusive yet irresistible "Fire in the Deep" that I hope to capture, however inadequately, in this second book of reflections upon the Word of God. It is my prayer and hope that *you* "catch fire" with the Word as so many others have before you.

However, before you begin your journey, I want to warn you of one thing: *DO NOT READ THIS BOOK unless you are willing to have the transforming fires of God's Spirit reshape every thought, desire, and motivation of your entire being!* Because once Love for the Lord flames up in your heart, once you allow the Spirit that appeared as *"tongues of fire"* to have free reign within you, you unleash a Fire not easily extinguished! You cannot know where your "Fire in the Deep" will lead you! (I guarantee it will be different than you have planned!) You cannot know what transformations in your spirit, what changes in your actions, will result. Once your spirit has been seared with the "glowing ember" of God's words, all other pleasures fade into the background. We can only say with Peter, "Where else can we go? You alone have the words of Life!" (see John 6:68)

Now that you have been forewarned, enjoy! May your deepest places burn with the Fire of the Almighty! May your soul be enflamed with the Passion of a Love that knows no boundaries! May your soul be seared by the Spirit of Truth and Freedom!

> "I have come to light a fire on the earth, and how I wish it were blazing!" (Luke 12:49–53)

—Robert Miller
August 2001

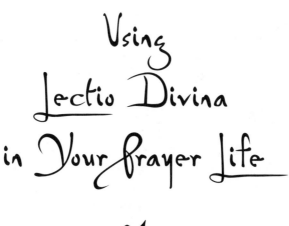

Using Lectio Divina in Your Prayer Life

This collection of lectionary-based Scripture meditations is written for a twofold purpose: to offer contemporary insights into the timeless wisdom of Scripture, and to inspire and deepen one's personal prayer and praise of our amazing God. In essence, these two purposes are what this time-honored tradition is all about.

As you commit yourself to the practice of *lectio divina*, you will want to establish a special place for your prayer time. This should be an area that is free of distractions and clutter, where you can sit comfortably and quietly for perhaps as long as thirty minutes. You will need a personal Bible (or some other source containing the full text of Scripture readings for that particular day) and any other items that help you enhance your sacred space (candles, notepad and pen, background music).

The practice of *lectio divina* consists of several simple steps. Following these steps in structuring your own meditations and Scripture study times will easily double the effectiveness and power of these times.

1. *Prepare yourself*
Mindfully enter your sacred prayer place and position yourself comfortably. As you mentally choose to clear your mind of worries, concerns, and pressures, center your thoughts and feelings upon God and his goodness to you.

2. *Read Scripture*

Open your Bible and locate the passages selected for the day. First, read the passages slowly and in their entirety, and let the message "sink into" your spirit. Then, read the passages (or parts of them) a second time, if you desire.

3. *Read the reflection*

Slowly read the reflection, pausing frequently to take in concepts. Allow them to challenge or soothe you while you pray spontaneously. This is not unlike "chewing" food; you turn words and phrases over and over in your mind as you pray and meditate on their import in your life. Allow words of prayer or praise to surface, and speak them to your God.

4. *Resolutions*

As you approach the end of your prayer time, conclude with silent resolutions or commitments of things you will attempt to do differently as a result of your meditation. Make these directly to your God. End with prayers of thanksgiving and gratitude for what God has done, is doing, and will yet do in your life. Again, completely place your life this day in God's hands.

People of Peace

First Sunday of Advent

(Isaiah 2:1–5)

"They shall beat their swords
    into plowshares,
    and their spears
        into pruning hooks" (Isaiah 2:4).
Historians say
    that in all recorded history,
    there have been
    only several hundred years
        without war or strife.
Left to ourselves,
    humans seem incapable
    of achieving this dream
    of universal peace
        and happiness.
Sad to say,
    humans do not know
    the way to peace.

Our archetypal human spirit,
    innately flawed by original sin,
    keeps this idyllic Isaiah vision
        only a distant, daring dream.

We far too easily choose
    fighting over negotiating;
    divorce and separation
        over dialogue and communication;
    selfish gratification
        over self-less service.
Sad to say,
    humans do not instinctively
    choose to be "people of peace."

Thus, as long as we inhabit
    this earthly plane of existence,
    we *need* to celebrate Christmas.
As this season nears yet again,
    our wounded world pauses
    to be reminded
    one more time
        about what peace is,
        where it is found,
        Who is its origin.
"Peace is my farewell to you,
    my peace I give to you,
    a peace the world cannot give" (John 14:27).

Jesus Christ was birthed
    into a broken, pain-full world
    that could not know Peace.
At his birth, angels sang
    "Peace on earth to those
    on whom his favor rests" (Luke 2:14).
Called the *"Prince of Peace,"*
    the Psalms prophesied of him
    "Justice shall flourish in his time,
    and profound peace,
    till the moon be no more" (Psalms 72:7).

To anyone who listened,
    and in a world that wouldn't care,

Jesus lived and taught
 the Peace that passes
 understanding.
He preached its potential
 to transform the human spirit,
 and he initiated its reign
  by signs and miracles.

Jesus promised Peace to us—
 not mere "surface peace"
  of smooth words
  and shallow actions,
 but the transformational inner Peace
  of knowing the Truth,
  hearing divine Wisdom,
  acting in justice and Love.
Jesus gave Peace to this world—
 healing wounded bodies,
 relieving burdened minds,
 revitalizing dashed dreams,
 anchoring broken spirits,
 energizing weary souls.
"I come that you may have Life—
 and have it to the fullest!" (John 10:10)

But most importantly,
 Jesus insisted that Peace
  not end with him.
Jesus commanded his followers
 to become people of peace.

Begin today to do that.
Bring the divine Peace
 present within
  into active practice
 in the world without.

Become a messenger of divine Peace,
    a voice for reason,
        harmony,
        goodwill,
        reconciliation,
    in this wounded world.

Be a model of patient love
    with your family.
Work at faithful communication
    with your beloved.
Develop a reputation
    for calm dialogue
        with co-workers.
Model peace-full ways
    of resolving conflicts
    with your neighbors.

Our model is the Master.
It is not that his Peace
    has failed or fallen short.
It is simply that
    it has never been tried.

A New World Order

Second Sunday of Advent

(Isaiah 11:1–10; Matthew 3:1–12)

"A shoot shall sprout
from the stump of Jesse,
from his roots
a bud shall blossom" (Isaiah 11:1).
Many years ago,
my father, brother, and I
spent an entire summer
clearing an overgrown lot
of sumac trees and debris.
As fast as the trees came down, however,
new shoots sprang up—
it was nearly impossible
to kill them off!

God's way of planning is similar.
At times, our life and struggles
may seem like a vacant lot
with old trees hewn down—
but this may be God's unique way
of clearing the ground
for a new world order.

When old, trusted trees fall,
   strange new shoots
      will suddenly spring up.

When old "kingdoms" collapse,
   the way finally becomes ready
      for a new Kingdom of Grace.
"A herald's voice in the desert:
   Prepare the way of the Lord!" (Matthew 3:3)

Perhaps the great mistake we make
   about the Creator's ways
   is failing to realize
      their radicalness.
God is not about "business as usual"
   in the human heart.
Jesus Christ does not want
   "just a few cosmetic changes."
The Spirit is not satisfied
   with a few saved souls
      in a vast uncaring world.
God has a radical new plan
   for transforming people
      and redeeming the world!
"What does this mean?
An entirely new teaching
   in a spirit of authority!" (Mark 1:27)

God's new world order begins with hope—
   that gentle Touch of divinity
      uplifting weary human frailty.
Where an old world sees dead stumps,
   God sees shoots of Life
      and sprouts of new beginnings.
Where an old world sees brokenness or death,
   God brings miracles
      of healing and Freedom.

"For my thoughts are not your thoughts,
says the Lord; nor are your ways
my ways" (Isaiah 55:8).

God's new world order
    empowers us to actually
        transform
        the old world order.
After "re-forming" our own attitudes,
        and redeeming our souls,
    God pours out the Fire
        of a new Spirit,
    "gifting" us to become
        witnesses of Life,
        agents of Peace.
"The spirit of the Lord shall rest on them,
    the Spirit of wisdom and understanding,
    the Spirit of counsel and of power,
    the Spirit of knowledge
        and fear of the Lord" (Isaiah 11:2).

God's new world order is about *Peace*—
    the Peace passing understanding,
        "a Peace this world cannot give."
This world's peace is fleeting,
    like "fast food" that leaves one
        hungry,
        unsatisfied,
    wanting more.
The Peace of God's inner touch
    fills our human hungers,
    satisfies our searching souls,
        makes the impossible possible.
"Then the wolf shall be
    a guest of the lamb,
    the leopard shall lie down
        with the kid;

the baby shall play
by the cobra's den" (Isaiah 11:5, 8).

Do not be unduly disturbed
   when seasons of change blow fiercely.
It is only when those "old trees"
   cluttering your vision and purpose
      are removed
   that a new vision for Life and Love
      can emerge.
Your Creator visions for you
   an entirely new way of Life.
The buds of this new world order
   are blossoming even now
      amidst the stubble of your fears.

Let God's Peace
   re-form you.
Let God's Power
   redeem you.
Let God's Hope
   renew you.
Let God's Fire
   rekindle you.

WEEK 3

Life out of Wilderness

Third Sunday of Advent

(Isaiah 35:1–6, 10; Matthew 11:2–11)

"The desert and the parched land
will exult . . .
they will bloom
with abundant flowers" (Isaiah 35:1).
Several years ago,
   in my inner-city home
     in Chicago,
   four public-housing buildings
   were demolished
     by implosion.
Plans are now in progress
   for 480 units
   of new mixed-income housing
   on that same spot.

Fifteen years ago,
   our parish church
   burned to the ground.
Now a new church building
   stands on the same spot,
   and new life,

energy,
    enthusiasm,
  has revitalized our church family.
Even in this "wilderness"
  of inner-city urban living,
    LIFE bursts forth!

We are seeing here
  in this physical realm
  what I have long seen
    in the spiritual realm:
  life comes in the wilderness!
The preeminent biblical message,
  the one constant theme
  in Deity embracing humanity,
    is simply this:
  God continually brings Life
  where wilderness and barrenness
    appear to reign!
"Jesus said to them
  'Go back and report to John
  what you hear and see:
  the blind recover their sight,
    cripples walk,
    lepers are cured,
    the deaf hear,
  dead men are raised to life'" (Matthew 11:4–5).

All through Scripture,
  God never ceases to surprise,
    even shock,
  by bringing Life out of death,
  new beginnings from old ruins.
Isaiah speaks prophetically today
  to a discouraged, demoralized people
  of deserts blooming,
    steppes rejoicing,
    the blind seeing.

In the prophet Ezekiel,
    even dry bones on a plain
    come snapping back together,
    and are filled with
        the Spirit of Life.

Gospel stories of Jesus' birth
    reveal the startling fact
    that the most unimportant village
        of the Old Testament
    becomes the birthplace
        for the New,
        the long-awaited Messiah.
In Matthew's story of Jesus,
    the enigmatic precursor of Jesus,
        John the Baptizer,
    comes out of the desert.
Jesus' own miracles
    are continual reminders that
        "with God,
        nothing will be impossible" (Luke 1:37).
Truly our God always
    finds a way
    to make a way
    where there is no way.
Indeed he *is* the Way.

Where today do you need
    new Life
        in the midst of old darkness?
What is your wilderness,
    your desert of dryness,
        depression,
        discouragement,
        disappointment?
Be reminded again this day
    that what may seem now
        to be a stumbling block

may soon become
    a stepping stone.
Be encouraged by the awesome fact
    that the Author of all Life
    is with you now,
        and that
    "the Word is near you,
        on your lips,
        in your heart" (Romans 10:7).

Meditate on this Word:
    "Here is your God,
        he comes with vindication . . .
        he comes to save you!" (Isaiah 35:4)
With your God,
    hopelessness becomes healing,
    weakness becomes strength,
    death becomes Life.
This is not just a promise.
This is Truth.

Messengers from God

Fourth Sunday of Advent

(Matthew 1:18–24)

"Joseph did as
  the angel of the Lord
  had directed him" (Matthew 1:24).
In recent years, angels
  have been "rediscovered"
    (although some would doubt
    they were ever lost).

There has been a surge
  of re-interest and fascination
  with these biblical beings
  who act so mysteriously
    throughout human history.
There are TV shows about them.
Books detail their role in life.
Pictures, pins, and jewelry
  adorn homes and hearts.

But the worst thing possible
  has happened to angels today:
  they have become "Hallmark-ized,"
    victims

of the reshaping
of modern mass media.
In the human rush to seize onto
   these safe, nonthreatening,
      omnipresent,
      otherworldly powers,
we stray from the Truth
   and Wisdom
of their biblical origins.

Angels are not magical protection
   against all evil in life.
Angels are not cute, fluffy beings
   whose powers humans gain
   by wearing their images
      on our clothing.
Angels are not ethereal entities
   detached from good or evil
   who flit about in time
   making humans feel cozy
      about themselves.

Angels are very real
   and really power-full.
Angels are without image or form,
   having being and substance
      as needed by their Maker.
Angels are "connected" beings,
   owing their onset and origin
      to God alone,
   receiving their entire purpose
      from God alone.
"The prayer was heard
   in the presence of Almighty God,
   so Raphael was sent
      to heal them both" (Tobit 3:16–17).

Although Scripture says some angels
   turned away from God,
     the vast host continue to carry out
        Divine actions
        by Divine command.
Some have been fiery warriors
   against evil and injustice
        (Michael in Daniel 12:1; Revelation 12:7).
Some act as companions on the journey,
   bringing healing and protection
        (Raphael in Tobit 5:4).
Some have acted as their name implies:
   "messengers" of sometimes shocking news
        (Gabriel in Daniel 9:21; Luke 1:19, 26).

"Such was his intention when suddenly
   the angel of the Lord appeared
      and spoke to him" (Matthew 1:20).
In the events surrounding Jesus' birth,
   God's angelic "fingerprints" abound.
Angels move, speak, and act literally
      "all over the place"—
   informing Mary,
   encouraging Joseph,
   singing praises to God,
   announcing to shepherds,
   protecting the newborn King
      (Matthew 2, Luke 2).

These amazing heavenly beings
   are indeed around today—
   still watching over us,
   still being used by God
   in the mysteriously unknowable ways
      of Divine Wisdom.
Although different than often portrayed,
   angels do move silently and subtly
      in this modern day and age—

witnessing to their Creator,
encouraging in quiet power,
empowering with divine guidance,
promising an eternal Presence,
reminding a skeptical age
    of eternal Truths.

We who are contemporary faith-seekers
    learn two great things
        from modern "angels."
First, God is best honored
    by a totally dedicated life—
    a life of praising God,
        honoring the Author of Life
    by thought, word, and deed.
The solitary focus of angels
    has always been
    that their Creator be glorified
        in every place,
        in every time.

Second, God's Power and Grace
    will always prevail.
The divine plan of Mercy and Love
    cannot be thwarted,
    and will be advanced,
        by any and all events.
Angels are divine reminders that
    "for those who love God,
    everything works out for good" (Romans 8:28).

Christmas Is Not Cute

Christmas

(Titus 2:11–14; Luke 2:1–14)

Chubby little baby Jesus
   with cute dimpled cheeks.
Sweet, pretty animals
   and well-dressed shepherds.
This is what manger scenes
   are generally made up of.
But make no mistake—
   the original Christmas
     was not a cute thing.

Christmas is not about
   a cute little baby
   in a chilly stable
     who loves everybody
     without exception.
This is only one truth
   of that amazing Birth
   that rocked the foundations
     of our universe.
Christmas is more accurately
   a radical statement
     about life's priorities.

Christmas is a radical restructuring
   of our vision of life and love.
"The grace of God has appeared,
   offering salvation to all people" (Titus 2:11).

In retelling this yearly story,
   there is a powerful message
   in the simple fact that
   today
   none of us knows a thing
   about the most powerful man
   in the world at that time—
      Caesar Augustus.
Yet, a simple baby
   born of itinerant, poor parents,
      in a foreign land,
   with no one around him—
   is now honored
      as the greatest human
      who ever lived!
Christmas turns all of life,
   its preconceptions,
      presumptions,
      prejudices,
   upside down!

Now this means several things
   for each of us.
First, your value and worth
   come from the inside
   not from external appearances,
      possessions,
      education.
God entered into you
   when he entered into the world.
"The Word of God is near you,
   in your heart,
      and on your lips" (Romans 10:8).

———

Know well your own value,
 your own innate goodness.
Look not to the world or others
 to give you the grace and beauty
 you already possess
 within yourself.
*"You are precious in my eyes
 and glorious,
 and because I love you"* (Isaiah 43:4).

Second, the world you live in
 takes on a different perspective
 because of Christmas Day.
This world is a beautiful place
 (God created it after all),
 but its values and priorities
 are completely
 out of order.
Live in this world,
 but do not be
 of this world.
*"Do not conform yourself to this world,
 but be transformed
 by the renewing of your mind"* (Romans 12:2).
Work hard in this world,
 play well, enjoy it fully,
 do what God calls you to do—
 but do not live for this world.
It is passing away.
Live for the world
 that will never pass away.

Lastly, the *way* you live
 can never be the same.
If this new year ahead
 is the same
 as every past "new" year,
 there is something wrong.

The birth of the God-child
    is a wake-up call
    to take God seriously
    in your life, work, play, loving.
Baby Jesus in a manger reminds us
    to carry the radical Christmas message
      of reversed priorities
    to all the world.

This "cute" baby Jesus
    was eventually killed
    by this world's powers.
But the world can never destroy
    the Power,
        Fire,
        Message,
        Vision of this *"Prince of Peace."*
"Peace on earth, good will to people"
    is the incredible Truth
    that turns this universe
      on its end.
May the Power of this day
    change your life forever.

Dare to Dream

Holy Family

(Matthew 2:13–15, 19–23)

"The angel of the Lord
   suddenly appeared
   in a dream" (Matthew 2:13).
Years ago, a popular song
   encouraged people to dream
     about "impossible dreams."
What are your
   "impossible dreams"?
For that matter,
   what are *your* dreams
   for yourself?
What are God's dreams
   for your life?

Dreams are essential
   for any healthy life
   (as research now confirms).
Dreams are God's way
   of breaking through
     human control and logic,
   of bringing the Divine
     into the merely human.

"When Jacob woke, he exclaimed,
 'Truly the Lord is in this spot,
 although I did not know it!'" (Genesis 28:16)

Whether in the fantastically
    phantasmic imagery of sleep,
        or the
    fully conscious commitment
    of inspired conviction,
    God-inspired dreams
    push the human spirit
        beyond itself,
    propelling us into
        insight and action.
"Because he had been warned in a dream,
    he departed for the region of Galilee" (Matthew 2:22).

Dreams and visions dominate
    the pages of Scripture.
Joseph heard God speaking
    in three separate dreams today.
Daniel's gift with dreams and visions
    changed kings and nations.
Isaiah's visions led to ministry,
    Ezekiel's challenged and confronted.
John saw heaven in his dream,
    Paul's dream gave discernment,
    Peter's changed the Church forever.
In all these dreams and visions,
    God's Voice was heard,
    God's Word was acted upon,
    God's Power was revealed.

"I will pour out my spirit on all.
Your sons and daughters shall prophesy,
    your old men shall dream dreams,
    your young men shall see visions" (Joel 3:1).

When you received God's Spirit,
   you received power to dream
      and courage to realize dreams.
How often do you allow
   God's "Spirit-world"
   to break into to your world?
Have you ever allowed your Self
   to receive an inner divine dream
      and be moved by it?
Have you ever let your spirit
   be pulled by God's Spirit
      into what *could* be,
      not what *has* to be?
Have you ever dreamed
   an "impossible dream"
   and paid the price
      for its fulfillment?

How well you personally
   act upon your dreams,
      responding to the mysterious Spirit,
      will likely determine
   the meaning, quality, and purpose
      of your entire life.
Do not be afraid
   to follow that Spirit,
      wherever it may lead.
Hold fast to the Anchor
   of God's historic Wisdom,
   but listen well
      for that Spirit-Dreamer
   speaking to you of
      new directions,
      needed changes,
      necessary losses.

Dare to dream!
"Impossible dreams" are only
   God's unrealized dreams.
By entering into our world,
   God's dreams have now
      become your dreams!
Dare to allow God's Wisdom
   to break through
      your limited logic.
Dare to become aware
   of another world attempting
      to expand your narrow vision.
Dare to say, as Dr. King did,
   "I have a dream!"
   and then have the courage
   to follow that dream
      wherever it leads.

Happy are those who
   dare to dream—
   and who are willing
      to pay the price
      to make those dreams
      come true!

Look Around You

Epiphany

(Isaiah 60:1–6; Matthew 2:1–12)

"Raise your eyes and look about . . .
you shall be radiant
at what you see" (Isaiah 60:4–5).
Michigan's state motto is:
"If you seek a beautiful place,
look around you."
The natural physical beauty
of my birthplace state
truly does make it
a water and winter wonderland.
But all of us would be blessed
if we daily remembered
that same motto.

For so many of us
walk through life
blind to God's beauty,
ignorant of divine gifts
around us everywhere.
For many, only until we meet
someone not able to see,
not able to hear or walk,

or when we ourselves
　　lose that gift,
do we fully appreciate
　　what is all around us.

Truly all we have is GIFT!
Despite the ugliness and sin
　　always pervading human society,
　　　　still the Gifting Grace of God
　　finds a way to break through.
Two thousand years ago,
　　King Herod plotted and schemed
　　　　against a simple baby—
　　yet God gifted the Holy Family
　　　　with safety,
　　　　peace,
　　and Magi visitors bearing gifts.
Ironically, these Eastern strangers
　　recognized the Gift among us
　　sooner than most locals did—
　　　　except for simple,
　　　　faith-filled shepherds.

"Raise your eyes and look about . . .
　　you shall be radiant
　　　at what you see."
Just as the Magi and shepherds
　　were "gifts" to Mary and Joseph,
　　　so God's amazing gifts
　　　and mysterious beauty
　　continue to be poured out today.
Even after presenting us
　　with the greatest Gift of all,
　　still our Creator
　　　just keeps on giving.
But seeing these divine gifts,
　　recognizing beauty around us
　　　depends upon us.

Do you have the insight and vision
    to see what many cannot?
Your human body alone is gift.
The capability of the human mind,
    its capacity to learn and recall,
    the dexterity of our body,
        its ability and agility—
    nothing humans have created
        can ever compare!
"A little less than the angels
    You have made us" (Psalms 8:6).

The awe of nature is astounding.
Powerful, ever-changing in its moods,
    how can anyone be blind
    to the stunning beauty of
        glorious red sunsets,
        snow-capped mountains,
        pristine clear-blue waters,
        primeval redwood stateliness,
        passionate raging storms?
"Praise the Lord from the heavens,
    praise him in the heights!" (Psalms 148:1)

The small gifts we so easily forget.
The kind word spoken providentially
    when we were lonely;
    that gentle embrace
        in a moment of aloneness;
    that kindness done to us
        just when we needed it;
    that Scripture or inspirational word
        coming when at our lowest.
"Then you shall be radiant at what you see,
    your heart shall throb and overflow" (Isaiah 60:5).

If you would see Beauty,
    look around you!

———

If you would find God,
   open your eyes and heart
     to see what
     you already see.
God is alive and well
   in his world today!

The signs of Power,
   the Gifts of God's Presence
     are all around!
"Epiphany" continues!
This day, along with the Magi,
   praise your Gifting God and say,
    "We have seen the signs
     and have come to adore the Lord!"(Matthew 2:2)

Has God Made a Difference?

Baptism of the Lord

(Isaiah 42:1–4, 6–7; Matthew 3:13–17)

Throughout history,
    many interesting people
        have received baptism.
Joseph Stalin, Jim Jones
    (of Guyana massacre fame),
    prominent mafioso figures,
    are but a few.
It is safe to say
    that the baptismal waters
    had little long-term effect
        on their actions.

It may sound like heresy,
    but simply being baptized
        is *not* enough.
The sacramental symbolism of
    pouring holy water
    over one's head
    does *not* suffice
        for salvation.

It is what God does
    in a person's heart—
    and what *you* do in response—
    that determines salvation.
The waters of baptism
    must be tested and proved
    in the fire
        of action and commitment.
"I am baptizing you in water . . .
    He will baptize you
    in the Holy Spirit and fire" (Luke 3:16).

When Jesus was baptized
    by his cousin John
        in the Jordan River,
    three things happened.
These same three things
    should also happen
        in us
    after our baptism.

First, his identity was affirmed.
Who Jesus was became clear—
    both to himself,
    and to the people
    (if they noticed).
"This is my beloved Son.
    My favor rests on him" (Matthew 3:17).
Many today seem not to know
    who they are.
Self-identity is a quest:
    anything that makes one feel good,
    anywhere you find it—
        it's all okay.
But baptismal rebirth gives you
    true and eternal identity.
God tells you who you are,
    makes you all you can be,

affirms you in what you will be.
"Here is my servant whom I uphold,
   my chosen one with whom
     I am pleased" (Isaiah 42:1).

Second, Jesus was empowered
   with a Fiery Spirit.
This Spirit strengthened him
   to heal powerfully,
     preach boldly,
      teach wisely.
"God anointed him
   with the Holy Spirit and power.
He went about doing good works
   and healing. God was with him" (Acts 10:37–38).
Your baptism empowers you, too,
   with a Fiery Spirit.
You have endless blessings
   and matchless power
     at your disposal!
Take strength for your fears,
   take courage in your doubts,
   take power when you are weak—
     all from the
   surpassing Spirit of God,
     who *"called you,*
     grasped you by the hand,
     formed you" (Isaiah 42:6).
Catch the Fire of the Lord!

Finally, Jesus was sent out
   on a life mission.
His baptism initiated
   a salvific ministry
     of love, freedom, and truth.
"He shall bring forth justice
   to the nations" (Isaiah 42:1).

As a result of your baptism,
    you, too, have a job to do,
    and a mission to undertake.
Your life mission is to act
    on what you say you believe.
It is to *"open the eyes of the blind"*
    by simple love and expectant faith;
    to *"bring out prisoners"*
        by witnessing to freedom and Truth;
    to touch *"those who live in darkness"*
        by gentle action
        and faith-full attitudes.

Stir up your baptism again!
Be re-baptized in Fire
    if not in water!
The "waters of Life"
    have indelibly etched
    the Lord's mark upon you.
Now allow that "Fire in the deep"
    to burn brightly
        for all the world to see!

The Two Greatest Days in Life

Second Sunday in Ordinary Time

(Isaiah 49:3, 5–6; 1 Corinthians 1:1–3; John 1:29–34)

A wise friend once told me
   that there are two great days
     in a person's life:
   the day you are born and
   the day you find out
     why you were born.
Most know that first day—
   people celebrate birthdays
     with parties,
     presents,
     friends.
But that second day
   is far more important.
It is that time when you find
   a purpose for your life,
     a reason for living—
   your destiny and vision,
     your "calling."
"It is too little for you
   to be my servant,
   I will make you a light
     to the nations" (Isaiah 49:5).

This second day is all about
   discovering a deeper meaning
   behind the tedium
     of life's treadmill.
It is that day when,
   reflecting on your gifts,
   you discern your destiny,
     and realize your purpose.
Throughout history,
   the greatest have been those
   who had that special sense
     of being "called."
"Paul, called by God's will
   to be an apostle of Christ Jesus . . ." (1 Corinthians 1:1).

Abraham, Moses, Samuel—
   all were ordinary people
   who heard a Divine call
     to *be* more and *do* more.
Francis of Assisi, Dorothy Day,
   Martin Luther King, Mother Teresa—
   all were just like you
   until that Fire within
     ignited their unique destiny.

The prophet Isaiah tells
   of his own special "second day"—
   "The Lord said to me:
     you are my servant,
     through whom I show my glory" (Isaiah 49:3).
Then John the Baptist speaks—
   "I saw the Spirit descend . . .
   Now I have seen for myself
     and have testified" (John 1:33–34).

How about you?
Have you celebrated
   that "second great day" yet?

Have you discovered
    your unique "destiny,"
    your purpose for being alive,
    your reason for rising daily?
Your birth date gave you Life,
    but your destiny date
        gives Power to live well.

The facts about you are this:
    you were formed and shaped
        by the divine Maker
        in your mother's womb.
When the "fullness of time" arrived,
    you were birthed into Life,
    placed with purpose and dignity
        into this universe.
You didn't earn this honor,
    you cannot pay for it—
    but you do have to accept it,
        and use it wisely.
Simply speaking, you are called
    to be different than
        the rest of world.
"The Lord called me from birth,
    from my mother's womb
        he gave me my name" (Isaiah 49:1).

Second, you need to discover
    just why you personally
        were given the Gift of Life.
What is your unique purpose,
    the reason you are here,
    the destiny only you
        can fulfill?
How were you meant to use
    that amazing gift of Life
        so freely granted you?

"I have plans for you—
  plans for your welfare,
    not your woe;
  plans to give you a future
    full of hope" (Jeremiah 29:11).

You were born with dignity.
You have been given much—
  so much will be expected of you.
You have an eternal destination—
  but a human destiny.
Pursue your life's purpose.
Dare to dream!

The World's Oldest Pastime

Third Sunday in Ordinary Time

(Matthew 4:12–23)

The world's oldest hobby
  is fishing.
Anthropologists say that
  for 500,000 years
  people fished or hunted
    to obtain food.
Only in the last five thousand years
  has humanity become agrarian.

Anyone who fishes regularly
  knows that fishing provides
  amazing insights
    into human character.
Herbert Hoover once said that
  "the surest way to know someone
  is to take him fishing."

This must be why Jesus Christ
  liked going fishing with
    prospective apostles.
I can well imagine the Master
  walking the shoreline of the

temperamental Sea of Galilee,
    watching them cast nets,
    drag the fish aboard,
    haul them ashore.
I can almost see him speaking
    as they rest from the day's work:
"Come and follow me,
    and I will make you
    fishers of men [and women]" (Matthew 4:19).

There was something solid,
    something deep and sure
    in these simple fishermen.
Jesus knew instinctively that
    His Kingdom could be established
    with such people as these.
"Upon this rock,
    I will build my church" (Matthew 16:18).
But what exactly did he see
    in these simple,
        uneducated,
        grimy fishermen ?
If we understand the Wisdom
    behind Jesus' choices,
    perhaps we ourselves can
        better respond to God
    in love and commitment.

First, Galilee fishermen
    were simple people,
        rooted people.
They were men of the earth,
    in touch with the basics of Life—
    the changing moods of seasons,
    the hard work survival requires,
    the deep faithfulness and passion
        of their life's calling.

They knew and respected both
the Creation they lived in,
and the Creator they worshiped.
Jesus seeks people in touch with
the simple "basics"
of Life and faith;
people not afraid
to stand up for them,
speak about them,
be passionate about them.
There is a simplicity to faith
that complicated minds
and brilliant theories
can never capture.

Second, the apostles possessed
patience and persistence.
When you fish, you learn
to sit still for hours—
waiting,
perhaps catching nothing.
With God, the race of life
is not to the swiftest,
strongest,
most successful,
most efficient.
The greatest Prize,
the ultimate "Big Catch,"
is won only by faithfulness.
Mother Teresa said it best:
"God did not call me
to be effective,
only to be faithful."

Lastly, the Galilee apostles
were not afraid to let others
see their faith.

They freely gave witness
   to the Fire that burned within them,
     the transformation God could do.
Although the preaching of Jesus
   initiated the Kingdom,
   it was the apostles' witness
   that nurtured and spread it.
It was their witnessing and preaching,
   their sacrificing and dying
   that brought faith
     to this generation.

Your faith must have an impact
   on others and the world.
Faith must be simple,
   faithful, and expressed.
What image of God do people see in you?
Do they say of you,
   "There is something different
     about this one"?
If you want to be a better Christian,
   imitate those Galilee fishermen.
Spend time fishing with the Master—
   in regular prayer and Scripture,
   in daily ministry
     and quiet faithful presence.
"Come follow me and I will make you
   fishers of the world!" (Matthew 4:19)

Blueprints for Life

Fourth Sunday in Ordinary Time

(1 Corinthians 1:26–31; Matthew 5:1–12)

A number of years ago,
   my sister and her husband decided
   to have a new house built.
A good contractor was found
   to draw up a well laid out
   set of blueprints.
From those essential plans,
   their entire house was built.
Today their house is beautiful—
   a well-designed building that is truly
   a home for their four children.

"Anyone who hears my words
   and puts them into practice
   is like the wise man
   who built his house on rock" (Matthew 7:24).

Blueprints are necessary
   for living a worthwhile life,
   as well as building a solid home.
The quality of life anyone leads,
   its ultimate purpose and meaning,

(and the judgment received on it)
depends greatly upon
the guidelines and blueprints
    we have laid out for ourselves
    and actually live by.

Early in his ministry,
    when Jesus was teaching,
    he laid out a clear set of
        "blueprints" or principles
    for living a faith-filled life.
Today they are called *beatitudes*,
    and they are principles of living
    unparalleled anywhere in literature.

"Blessed are the poor in spirit . . ."
"Poor" does not mean
    a lack of possessions
        or absence of wealth,
    so much as it means
        relying upon God
        to provide for all our needs.
We independent, self-reliant Americans
    have a great lesson to learn here.
The *reign of God* belongs only
    to those who realize
        that freedom and independence
    must be balanced
        by absolute dependence
        on a Higher Power.
The truly wise work for their bread,
    but look to the Lord for *daily bread,*
    and are "rich" enough
        to be "poor" in the Lord.

"Blessed are those who show mercy . . ."
Blessed are those people generous
    with what they have and are,

those who are not stingy or cheap
 with their acts of kindness,
who do not hoard their life and gifts
 but freely share
 their time, talents, and treasure.
"God chose those
 whom the world considers absurd
 to shame the wise" (1 Corinthians 1:27).

"Blessed are the single-hearted . . ."
It is a special gift
 to be able to focus on
 truly important things in life.
Most of us today get so caught up
 with the stress and pressure
 of life's worries and problems
that we lose that single-minded focus
 so key to true happiness.
In the end, all that matters
 is your ability to focus—
to see the real treasures of life,
 not obsess on the trappings
 people surround themselves with.
"There are but three things that last . . ."
 (1 Corinthians 13:13).

"Blessed are the lowly [meek] . . ."
This concept has absolutely no relevance today.
It connotes weakness or wimpiness,
 implies softness or fear.
But "lowly" in Jesus' time
 meant the inner power
 of holding all life-forces,
 all personal energies
 in balance.
It refers to the difference between
 living in reckless excess
 or healthy balance.

"Not by might, nor by strength,
    but by my Spirit, says the Lord" (Zechariah 4:6).

Following God's blueprints in life
    will build a beautiful mansion as well—
    an eternal mansion in heaven!
Blessed are you who do this,
    "be glad and rejoice,
    for your reward in heaven is great!"

Can "Vogue" Models Enter Heaven?

Fifth Sunday in Ordinary Time

(Isaiah 58:7–10; 1 Corinthians 2:1–5)

Our world today seems obsessed
   by attributes of physical beauty.
The women of *Vogue*, the men of *GQ*—
   these are advertisers' role models
   for what many consider
   beauty and attractiveness
     to be.
But it is not physical appearance
   that makes for true beauty;
   nor do looks and strength
   make one appealing to God.
"As for myself, when I came to you,
   I did not come
   with any particular eloquence
     or 'wisdom'" (1 Corinthians 2:1–5).

Indeed, throughout history,
   some of life's most famous people
   were not physical beauties.

Charles Steinmetz,
   the genius of electricity,
   was a hunchback,
     almost a dwarf.
Thomas Aquinas,
   the great Catholic theologian,
   was called by his confreres
     "the dumb ox."
Jesus Christ himself
   according to Scripture
   had *"in him no appearance*
   that would attract us to him" (Isaiah 53:2).

God does not see shape, size,
   health, success, or money
   when judging the quality,
     value, or worth of people.
The One who created all things
   has criteria for beauty
     much deeper
   than creation judges itself by.
Beauty in the Real World of eternity
   springs from inner aspects
     not outer appearances.

God's "beautiful people"
   are not famous movie stars,
   well-dressed, wealthy prominents,
   athletes with attitudes,
   well-toned, health-club fiends,
   pop-icon rock stars and musicians,
     or gorgeous runway models.
"As for those who seemed to be important—
   whatever they were
   makes no difference to me.
   God does not judge
     by external appearance" (Galatians 2:6).

Our Creator-God describes his own
  perfect ideal of beauty
    in Isaiah 58—
  those who *"share their bread*
    with the hungry,
  shelter the oppressed
    and the homeless,
  remove from their midst
    oppression,
    false accusation,
    malicious speech" (Isaiah 58:6–9).
Divine standards of true beauty
  focus instead on
  the just actions
    of convicted hearts,
  the unselfish thoughts
    of humbled spirits,
  the deep wisdom
    of the poor in spirit.
"Your faith rests not on the wisdom of men,
  but on the power of God" (1 Corinthians 2:5).

What impresses our God
  is not outer physical beauty,
  fancy cars, clothes, or jewelry—
  lifestyles "of the rich and famous"—
  but rather the inner spiritual beauty of
    a humble heart,
    a willing spirit,
    an unselfish mind.
"My message had none
  of the persuasive force
    of 'wise' argumentation,
  but the convincing power
    of the Spirit" (1 Corinthians 2:4).

It is not what you *do*
    (accomplishments, success, wealth)
    or you *are* by yourself
    (looks, talent, beauty)
      that matters in the end.
It is rather what *God* can do
    through you
      when you allow God to.
Work on developing inner beauty.
Fill your Self with a Love
    that is beyond this world.
Follow the deep Wisdom
    of the Spirit within you.
Forge an identity based
    on inner values
      rather than outer appearances.
"Greater is He that is in you
    than he that is in the world" (Philippians 4:13).

Valentine's Day Love?

Sixth Sunday in Ordinary Time

(Matthew 5:17–37)

Love.
It is the greatest gift
   of a passionate God
   to his precious people.
It is the anchor,
   the necessary rock
   of any healthy and happy life.
We all need to be loved
   and to love.

But here again,
   our society seizes "love"
   and suborns it
     for its own purposes.
Even this greatest God-given Gift
   has been trivialized,
     institutionalized,
     commercialized.
Valentine's Day is a beautiful feast,
   named after an ancient saint.
But this fourth-century bishop
   would turn in his grave

if he could see how his name
   is being misused today.

In the person of Jesus Christ,
   God modeled for us "true love,"
   pushing us beyond the "love"
of cheap cards, romance novels, easy sex,
   to something much deeper.
"Unless your holiness surpasses
   that of the Scribes . . ." (Matthew 5:20).
The love that fires the Spirit
   of a person dedicated to God
   is different from the love
     the world inundates us with.

A person serious about spirituality
   must do more and love better
     than the rest of the world,
   for our role model is One
   who paid the ultimate price
     for true Love—
   giving up life itself
     for the ones he loved.
"As the Father has loved me,
   so I have loved you.
     Live on in my love" (John 15:9).

"You have heard the commandment,
   'You shall not commit murder.'
   I say, everyone who grows angry
     will be liable to judgment" (Matthew 5:21–22).
True Love goes far beyond
   the bare minimums.
Do not say of yourself,
   "I haven't murdered anyone,
   I haven't slept around,
   I haven't stolen."

Rather, examine the inner attitudes
   of the secret places
      of your heart.
Examine your patterns
   of intimate loving
   by using scriptural wisdom.
"Love is patient, kind,
   doesn't boast, is not proud,
    not rude, not self-seeking" (1 Corinthians 13:4–5).

"You have heard it said,
   'You shall not commit adultery.'
   I say, whoever looks at a person lustfully
   has already committed adultery . . ."
     (Matthew 5:27–28).
The barest minimum of committed love
   is faithfulness to one's beloved.
Yet Jesus pushes believers
   beyond the minimum.
The deepest intimacy and highest ecstasy
   humanly possible for two people
  comes *not* from sexual actions
    done in private,
   but from the deep friendship
    of shared mutual support,
   the intimacy of two hearts
    made one by unselfish sharing.
An old couple once said,
   "It is far more important for two people
  to be good friends
  than it is for them
   to be good lovers."

"Say 'yes' when you mean yes,
   and 'no' when you mean no" (Matthew 5:37).
Love is not a feeling

but a decision one makes.
All true Love demands a choice,
   requiring people to choose Love
      again and again,
      each and every day.
Love is not upheaving emotions
   or physical experience,
   nor an easily acquired
      state of happiness.
True Love is renewed daily,
   made fresh each morning.
True Love is mutual honesty,
   personal integrity,
      mutual forgiveness.
True Love transforms a person,
   turning one upside down.
True Love affects deep attitudes,
   changing mere surviving
      into Real Living.

And the greatest lover
   is the most committed,
      most unselfish,
      faith-full lover—
   like the Lover
      who loved us into Life.
Let your Love surpass
   that of the world.

"I Don't Get Mad, I Get Even"

Seventh Sunday in Ordinary Time

(Leviticus 19:1–2, 17–18; Matthew 5:38–48)

If you drive a car,
    you have probably seen it.
It is a bumper sticker proclaiming
    a "tough guy" attitude—
    "I don't get mad,
        I get even."
The phrase sums up well
    the attitude many adopt
    to this world's difficulties—
    aggressive and assertive,
        "in your face,"
        tit-for-tat.

I have a very difficult time
    seeing Jesus Christ
    plastering that sticker
    across any car he might drive.
I cannot imagine even Peter,
    the reactionary and assertive
        leader of the Twelve,
    espousing this philosophy

as he preached
    throughout Galilee.
Jesus Christ taught humans
    to respond differently
        to evil in this world,
        to personal challenges
        and unforgiveness.

In his most difficult,
    most challenging teaching,
    Jesus offered a truly radical
        Life approach:
"You have heard the commandment,
    'An eye for an eye,
        a tooth for a tooth,'
    but what I say to you is:
        offer no resistance to injury" (Matthew 5:38–39).
Our higher Power knew well
    the power, depth, and scope
        of Evil—
    what it does,
    how it corrupts and pollutes
        the human spirit.
The Son of God himself was killed by Evil
    in both personal
    and institutional forms.

But the One called Prince of Peace
    knew that such a negative force
    could only be confronted
    by a more powerful opposite force—
        the Power of Love.
"Perfect love casts out fear" (1 John 4:18).
So Jesus taught his followers
    to respond with Love
        in the face of Evil—
    not to retaliate
        or act with vengeance,

but to conquer
by standing firm
   in a greater Power.

The Power of patient Love,
   of stubborn, persistent,
      nonviolent Love
is awesome
   and utterly disarming.
With such nonaggressive Power,
   Gandhi stared down British imperialism
      early in the twentieth century.
With such patient Power,
   Martin Luther King, Jr., and others
   confronted and defeated
   racism and prejudice
      in the 1960s.

In the face of the "dark sides"
   of this modern world—
   injustice and terrorism,
   greed and selfishness,
      the evils of hate and denial—
   making conscious choices
   for nonviolent,
      nonaggressive Love
is always the wiser
course of action.
Divine Wisdom has shown
   again and again
   that the Power of Love
   defeats the "dark powers"
      of Evil and hate.

But Love is always a choice.
The choice of a basic Life attitude
   is in your hands alone—
   bitterness or benevolence,

aggression or nonviolence,
    love or hate.
"Choose this day whom you will serve" (Joshua 24:15) .

Choose to respond with gentleness
    in the face of anger and bitterness.
Choose to respond with Love
    in the face of frustration and discouragement.
Choose to stand firm and unmoving
    in the face of injustice,
    acting with courage
        to confront prejudice.

Choose Love,
    and you choose to *"be perfect*
    as your heavenly Father is perfect."
Love completes one's Self,
    and begins to make whole
    the broken pieces
        of our fractured world.

Leaning on Everlasting Arms

Eighth Sunday in Ordinary Time

(Isaiah 49:14–15; Matthew 6:24–34)

It is a classic movie scene—
   the final farewell,
     one person looking longingly
       at the departing beloved,
     saying with tears in eyes,
       "I will never forget you!"
Perhaps you personally have memories
   of such poignant promises of
     ongoing love,
     unending devotion,
     eternal remembering.

But the hard reality is that
   human love does not always
     last forever.
What starts as great romance
   often ends as great tragedy.
Promises of eternal faithfulness
   turn into painful accusations
     of forget and neglect.
Vows of commitment too often
   lead to papers of separation.

But while mere human love
   so often seems to disappoint
     or be lacking,
     or always fall short,
   there is one Love
   that never fails
     never frustrates,
     never abandons.
It is the Love of the One
   who brought you into this world,
   who sustains you each day,
   who is closer than you are
     to your Self.

The prophet Isaiah sums up so well
   the archetypal fear and hope
   of our human spirit.
"Zion says, 'The Lord has forsaken me,
   my Lord has forgotten me'" (Isaiah 49:14).
 How often have these been
   your own exact sentiments?
How frequently have you yourself
   cried out in spirit,
     "Where are you, my God?
     Why am I so alone here?"
How deeply does Isaiah's cry
   of being forsaken and forgotten
   resonate in your own spirit?

But to our wounded, lonely spirit,
   our Creator God cries out in response.
"Can a mother forget her infant,
   or be without tenderness
     for the child of her womb?" (Isaiah 49:15)
How often have you heard a mother
   suddenly slap her forehead and say,
   "Oh my, I forgot about
   that third child of mine!

I wonder what she is up to now."
Impossible!
No mother ever forgets
   a child carried within her
      for nine intimate months!

The same logic applies to Abba,
   your Creator-God
   who is both Father and Mother
      to you.
"Even should she forget,
   I will never forget you!" (Isaiah 49:15)
Your God is so deeply
   in love with you
   that God danced
      the day you were born!
Your God craves your presence daily,
   searching the day long
   to hear simple word
      or thought.
The One who created you
   could no more forget you
   than the Creator could forget
      his own Son Jesus!

As you wander through
   life's wandering ways,
   learn well the art of leaning,
      of leaning on Everlasting Arms.
Lean not on any other human
   to satisfy and satiate
      your deepest cravings.
Lean not upon this world's gifts
   to fill up those nagging gaps
      in your human condition.
Lean not out of frustration
   solely upon your own
      embittered inner Self.

Rather, lean daily upon the One
 whose Love never fails.
Lean upon the One who
 never forgets you,
 never abandons you,
 never forsakes you.

Spend time this day
 practicing your leaning!
Lean upon the deep Wisdom,
 and rest in the deep Peace
  of these words and promises.
"Do not worry.
Look at the birds of the sky.
They do not sow or reap,
 yet your heavenly Father feeds them.
Are you not more important than they?

"Stop worrying!
Your heavenly Father knows
 what you need.
Seek first God's kingship over you,
 and all these things
  will be given you besides!"

Temptation and Testing

First Week of Lent

(Genesis 2:7–9, 3:1–7; Matthew 4:1–11)

In 1923, at Chicago's Edgewater Hotel,
   nine men gathered.
These were no ordinary men,
   but the most powerful,
   most influential men
    in America.
Present that day
   were bank and major corporate presidents,
   a presidential cabinet member,
   the head of the New York Stock Exchange.

From a human perspective,
   these men had power and prestige,
   were the epitome of success.
But God does not value
   what the world values.
From a divine perspective,
   these man were facing
   the greatest temptations
   the world has to offer.

The word *temptation* means
    to be tested and tried,
    to have one's eternal values
        confronted,
        challenged,
        questioned.
Throughout life,
    every human must sound the depths,
    test the extent of his or her
        personal beliefs and values.
Even the Master
    was not free from temptation.
Jesus Christ had to face
    severe tests and challenges
    from his greatest enemy—
    the one called "Satan"
        (the Adversary).
In Jesus' temptations,
    we find our own mirrored as well.

Matthew tells us that Jesus was tempted first
    to change stones to bread.
This was a test to convince him
    to take care of himself first,
    to accumulate earthly things,
        and thus
    satisfy his own personal needs
        ahead of any others.
Jesus' response was from Scripture,
    and reaffirmed that nothing
    this world can offer
    fully satisfies the human heart.
"Not on bread alone is man to live,
    but on every utterance that comes
        from the mouth of God" (Matthew 4:4).

———

Next, his Adversary set Jesus
   atop the great Temple,
      tempting him
   to manifest his power
   by inviting angels
      to magically appear,
   saving him from a great fall.
This was a test of pride and power,
   a subtle invitation to glorify himself
      and misuse his sacred powers.
Jesus, however, resists this lure
   of grandiose ego-inflation,
   warning his Adversary
      about the dangers
   of pushing the boundary of Divinity.
"You shall not put
   the Lord your God
      to the test" (Matthew 4:7).

Lastly, the Evil One confronts Jesus
   with kingdoms of money, power,
      grandeur, and fame—
   promising them to him if only
   Jesus acknowledged the Evil One's primacy.
This was a test of life-priorities,
   a question of ultimate worship
      and intrinsic values—
   who or what do you worship in life?
What is the "lord" of your life?
Jesus immediately saw through
   these tempting illusions.
"You shall do homage
   to the Lord your God;
      him alone shall you adore" (Matthew 4:10).

Jesus faced his temptations well—
   but how have you done with yours??

———

The final words of this Gospel
 are most intriguing.
"The devil left him"—
  but not forever!
Both with Jesus and ourselves,
 the Adversary is never
  too far away.

Face your temptations well today—
 with searing sincerity,
  divine trust,
  battle-tested wisdom.
Your own "Adversary" may well return
 even stronger the next time.

Oops, I am sorry.
I never concluded my opening story.
Twenty-five years after that 1923 meeting
 in a prominent Chicago hotel,
three of these important men
  had committed suicide,
 three others
  had gone bankrupt,
 two more
  were in prison,
 and one man
  died insane.
It would seem they were tested
 and found wanting.
May you not be.

The Heartbeat of Faith

Second Week of Lent

(Genesis 12:1–4; Matthew 17:1–9)

"You have made man
    a little less than angels . . ." (Psalms 8:6).
Of all the anatomical parts
    of our amazing human body,
        the most fascinating
            and vital
        is the human heart.
Medical people tell us
    the heart operates
        in a twofold process.
First, in the diastolic process,
    the heart dilates and expands,
    and the chambers fill up with blood.
Then, in the systolic process,
    the heart contracts,
    and blood is pumped and forced
        outwards,
    back into the body.

This utterly essential
   "in and out" action
   forms the heartbeat
     of all human life.
When the process fails,
   humans suffer heart attacks,
   dangerous arrhythmia,
     blood clots.

The world of the spiritual
   often parallels the physical.
This same twofold anatomic process
   can be seen
   in our spiritual life journeys.
There is a time for drawing in,
   for filling up one's resources,
   taking in the spiritual energy,
     the personal power
   needed to survive.
This "spiritual diastolis"
     is seen in Matthew 17 today.

Jesus has been ministering,
   healing, preaching, teaching,
     throughout Galilee.
Now he takes his three friends
   and withdraws up a mountain
     to pray,
     to meditate,
   to enter into quiet time
     with his Father.
This retreat becomes a time
   of personal Transfiguration.
The prayer space around the four
   is transformed into
     Holy Ground.

They experience a revelation,
   a divine manifestation,
   that empowers and changes them
    forever.
"This is my beloved Son
   on whom my favor rests.
Listen to him" (Matthew 17:5).

For ourselves as well,
   it is vital to take time away,
   time to "draw back"
    and draw into ourselves
   the spiritual life-blood of God's
    peace, wisdom, Spirit.
Simply stated, it is impossible
   to become a spiritual person
   without sitting quietly
    before your God.

But after "drawing in" Peace,
   there is a need
    for "systolic spirituality"—
   for going back out into the world,
    witnessing to others,
    acting in faith.
In Genesis 12, the Lord speaks
   of this "going out" need to Abraham.
"Go forth from your homeland
   to a new land
    that I will show you.
I will make of you a great nation,
   and I will bless you" (Genesis 12:1–2).

All through Scripture,
   God always tells people
    "where to go"—

Abraham, Moses, Joseph,
Peter, Paul, and many others.
Today, as well, God needs people
    willing to be used
    as messengers and witnesses
        to this unbelieving world.
The Word of God is only spread
    by people like you—
    who get involved,
    who act on the faith
        God has given them,
    who step out
        despite their fears and doubts.

Diastolic and systolic actions:
    together these make up
        the heartbeat of life,
        and the rhythm of faith!
Take a close look
    at your spiritual life.
There should be systolic times
    of ministry, mission, and work
    in your community, family, and church.
Jesus did say in Matthew 25
    we would be judged
        by such acts of love.
But to be energized and effective,
    there must also be diastolic times
        of restoration,
    in-filling,
        personal renewal.
Take time away to light that
    "fire in the deep"—
    then move out to spread
        that fire of God
        to all you meet.

Waters of life

Third Week of Lent

(Exodus 17:3–7; John 4:5–42)

Few things in American life
   are more taken for granted
      than water.
This precious life-giving commodity
   is like gold to some—
   but it is used recklessly
   to brush teeth, wash cars,
      drink beverages, cook,
      clean ourselves,
      and much more.
But in the desert surroundings
   of the biblical world,
   water became a key part
   of how God taught his people.

As the Israelites crossed the Red Sea,
   finally freed from Egypt,
   there was exultation and joy.
But wandering in the desert,
   "in their thirst for water,
   the people grumbled against Moses
   saying,

'*Why did you ever make us leave Egypt?*'" (Exodus 17:3)
In their complaining and mistrust,
   they refused to see how God
   could still be with them.

But then came the lesson.
   Suddenly God brought forth water
   from the last place they expected—
     the middle of a rock!
The "waters of life"
   came from the rocks of despair.

Is it not true with ourselves
   that at the rocks of our own
     frustration,
     disappointment,
     weariness,
   we, too, often begin to doubt,
     even question God?
Where is God?
Why does he not act?
Why does life seem so long,
   and the journey so dry?

But God responds today
   as God always has;
   and God's words are eternal
     and true:
"Have I brought you this far
   only to abandon you?
You haven't even *begun* to look yet!
Hit that rock—and trust me!"

Today, Jesus uses the need for water
   to teach and challenge
     another troubled person.
Breaking an established taboo
   of talking with a single woman,

Jesus challenges her
    with hard life-questions.
"He told me everything I ever did" (John 4:29).
Then he offers her *his* water—
    "The water I give shall become
      a fountain of life,
    leaping up to provide eternal life" (John 4:14).

Just as water dripping incessantly
    alters the strongest rock,
    just so
      will the Living Water of Jesus
    inevitably alter
    your entire existence.
No hidden part of your Self
    can remain untouched—
    as the Samaritan woman's revelation
    of past failed relationships indicates.

Where are those personal barriers,
    those rocks of despair,
      in your life this day?
Where do you need
    the Living Waters of Jesus
    running over,
      through,
      around,
    the rocks of your fears,
      faults,
      failures?
Where do you need
    to strike the rock—
      and believe?

Allow the Water of God's Life
    to wash over your entire being,
    to flow through the rocks
    of your life—

cleansing guilt,
washing away fear,
restoring hope.
"Whoever drinks the water I give
   will never be thirsty" (John 4:13).

Walk through the deserts
   of this temporary abode
      with absolute trust
   in the unseen eternal Waters
      awaiting you.
Trust in God's Presence
   despite not always seeing
      the "big plan."

"Hit the rocks" blocking your path
   with utter faith
      and complete confidence—
   knowing that *"with God*
      all things are possible."
"Hit the rocks"
   and expect God's Water of Life
      to flow freely.

And then, pause to drink deeply.
Drink in the refreshment,
   the renewing,
      that only your God
         can give.

Who Is Really Blind?

Fourth Week of Lent

(Ephesians 5:8–14; John 9:1–41)

For many unending years,
    a blind man used to sit begging
    at a busy downtown Chicago intersection.
The poor man was a contrast
    to those moving around him—
    wealthy, busy,
        self-important people
    who walked by him daily.
Most looked at him as a
    flawed, broken,
        blind individual.

But who was *really* blind here?
Was it this blind beggar man
    or those walking by
        who had eyes
        but could not see?
Instead of feeling pity,
    sorrow, scorn, or disdain
    for the begging of a blind man,
        perhaps

those people
should have examined themselves first
    for their own blindness.

In the Gospel today,
    who did Jesus get upset with?
Certainly not the man born blind—
    his disability *"was no sin,*
    either of this man or his parents" (John 9:3).
Jesus can and did easily heal
    physical blindness.
It is the blindness
    of closed minds,
        personal discrimination
        and prejudicial attitudes
    that is the greater problem.
"If you were blind,
    there would be no sin in that.
'But we see,' you say,
    and your sin remains" (John 9:41).

Clearly, Jesus' main concern here
    are those who think they see
        when they do not.
Unfortunately, this type of blindness
    is rampant today
    and has many shapes and forms:
        racism in housing and jobs,
        prejudices of color or sex,
        intolerance in faith and religion,
        smug self-righteous attitudes,
    and their many subtle variations.

However, the core spiritual problem
    behind any twentieth-century American blindness
        is denial and ignorance.

Just as in Jesus' time,
   those most guilty
      are those most unaware.
"Some of the Pharisees said to him
   'Surely we are not also blind,
      are we?" (John 9:40)

Denial exists in people's motives.
"I don't have a problem
   with 'those people.'
I'm just moving
   for the better schools."
Ignorance of economic realities abounds.
   "'Those people' should just
      go and get jobs."

Prejudice knows no race, color, or sex.
"The white man is no friend
   of the black man."
"That's not a woman's place."
"I can never be at peace
   with that Jew . . .
      that Arab . . .
      that foreigner."

Blind to the presence of Blessings,
   some choose only to see problems.
"Why does pain and suffering exist
   if God is so good and loving?"
"I have to take care of myself first,
   'cause no one else will."

Reflect this day on the blindness,
   denial, and ignorance
   which may reside in you.

Think carefully about the wisdom
   spoken by Richard Rohr:
   "Every viewpoint
     is a view
     from a point."
Never allow your personal life "view"
   to become too narrow because
   your "point" does not include
     certain people,
     places,
     experiences,
   different from your own,
   but important to God.

"For you were once darkness,
   but now you are light in the Lord.
Live as children of light.
Light produces every kind
   of goodness, justice, and truth" (Ephesians 5:89).
As a child of Light,
   there is no place for darkness,
   no room for any shadows
     that cast blindness.
The Light of God within is intended
   to shine everywhere,
   in every circumstance,
     to every person.

Allow the Light to illumine
   every darkness and denial.
Pray for the grace
   of an open mind
     and a flexible spirit,
   so that you, too, can say,
"I once was blind,
     but now I see" (John 9:25).

Love Conquers All

Fifth Week of Lent

(Ezekiel 37:12–14; John 11:1–45)

The blockbuster movie *Titanic*
   highlighted two young people
   whose love surpassed the years.
Theirs was a love so strong
   that even the sinking
      of that great ship
   and the physical end of life
      could not conquer it.
True Love is never diminished—
   even by the losses of life,
   or the loneliness of death.

There probably is nothing
   more feared and unknown
      than death.
Consider all the pills taken,
   the airplanes not flown in,
   the regular checkups taken,
   the fat jogged off,
      and, in general,

all the things people do
to insure a long life
and avoid death.

Death is the great unknown.
It is the silent angel
awaiting everyone—
rich and poor,
powerful or powerless.
Yet, into the midst of this,
our greatest fear,
walks Jesus Christ
with the greatest Peace
any human can experience.
"If you believe in me,
you will never die" (John 11:26).

These words are a promise
that only Someone
passionately in love
would make.
"I do not want to lose you!
Where I am, you also will be!
You will live forever!"
"'Your brother will rise again,'
Jesus assured her" (John 11:23).

It astounds me personally
that Someone (*anyone!*)
could care for me that much—
to promise me
that I will be with him
forever,
if only I follow him
faithfully.
This amazing man, Jesus Christ,
whom we follow, trust, and love,
is indeed deeply moved

by the pains and losses
    of our journeys
        through this world.
He is moved because
    he is in love—with us!
"He was troubled in spirit,
    moved by the deepest emotions . . .
    which caused the Jews to remark,
    'See how much he loved him!'" (John 11:33–36)

Today God makes a promise
    that can only be made
    by One burning with love,
        fired by passionate intimacy.
To any God-Lover
    who believes completely,
        and loves sincerely,
    our Beloved promises
    that death will never end
        the Love you share;
    that Life will continue on,
        changed,
        perfected,
        for all eternity.
And, you see, this Lover,
    this man, this Jesus,
    has the Power
    to back up his words!
"I am the resurrection and the life,
    whoever believes in me,
    even though he should die,
        will come to life . . .
    Do you believe this?" (John 11:26)

Do you believe that your God
    is so in love with you
    that his love can conquer
        all fear in your life?

Do you believe that he can
    "roll away the stones"
        of your concerns,
    terrors,
    problems,
    worries?
Do you believe you can be loved
    in such an amazing way?
"Because you are precious in my eyes,
    and because I love you!" (Isaiah 43:4)

Let the awesome reality
    of passionate Divine Love
    sink into your psyche today.
Let God's unending Love
    transform your entire vision
        of living and thinking—
    so that no fear remains,
        only Love and action.
Rest in the astonishing reality
    that Someone thinks enough of you
        to say,
    "I will open your graves
    and have you rise from them.
    I will put my spirit in you
        that you may live,
    and I will settle you
        upon your land.
    I have promised,
        and I will do it!" (Ezekiel 37:13–14)

Jesus Dies Today

Palm Sunday

(Philippians 2:6–11; Matthew 26:14–27:66)

The author Elie Wiesel,
    a concentration camp survivor,
    tells a story about his prison.
Following the attempted escape
    of several prisoners,
    all the men were lined up
    to watch the hanging
    of a number of others—
        in retaliation.
As the bodies dangled in the air,
    one prisoner cried out,
    "Where is God now?"
From the back of the lines,
    a muted voice responded,
      "He is hanging from that rope
      right now."

As the death of Jesus Christ
    is retold so powerfully
      this sacred day,
    the reality of sacrificial,
      redemptive death

may be quite difficult
   for us modern-day Christians
      to relate to.
No one in America
   dies for their faith today—
   indeed, few seem willing
   to truly "give" their life
   for *anything* of real substance
      or deep significance.

Yet, the death of Jesus Christ
   continues to be
      the defining Reality
   for any believer.
No one calling himself or herself a believer
   can enter heaven's gates
   without confronting that event,
      and
   walking through his death
      in a very real way.
"I have been crucified with Christ,
   and the life I lead is not my own" (Galatians 2:19).

What may be surprising to you
   is the fact that Jesus
   continues to die
      today.
Jesus dies and Life results—
   in countless ways
   and in innumerable actions
      of self-giving
      every day.
"Your attitude must be Christ's:
   though he was in the form of God,
   he did not deem
      equality with God
   something to be grasped at.
   Rather, he emptied himself . . ." (Philippians 2:6).

The utterly unselfish health care
   some people give
   to family members
     in their final days—
   Jesus dies, and Life flows.

The bold courage of those
   who take value-based stands
   in difficult moral circumstances—
   Jesus dies, and Life flows.

The quiet, daily faithfulness
   of those who choose
   a gentle response to anger
     instead of
   a vengeful retort—
   Jesus dies, and Life flows.

The slow dying to Self
   of those courageous ones
     who serve others
   in service professions
     or ministry outreach
   without thought of personal reward—
   Jesus dies, and Life flows.

The very real martyrdom
   of hundreds of
   faith-filled believers
   on other continents
   whose lives were not as important
   as the values they stood for—
   Jesus dies, and Life flows.

No believer leaves this world
   without dying—
   both literally
     and figuratively.

But the "deaths" we willingly choose
    before our final day
    will be the most significant.
"If we have died with him,
    we shall also live with him" (Romans 6:8).
By laying down our life
    in acts of love,
        courage and conviction,
    we, too, walk into new Life.

Can you say with Peter today,
    "Even though I have to die
        with you,
    I will never disown you"? (Matthew 26:35)
Or do you betray Jesus again by
    indecision,
    lack of faithfulness,
    lack of moral courage
        in crisis times,
    self-focused desires
        for security and safety?

Could you die for Jesus today?

Reflect long on the fact
    that Jesus already did—
        for you.

Walk in the Light

Easter

(John 20:1–9)

Several years ago,
   after years of illness,
   my mother
     went to her eternal reward;
   or as my community would say,
   she "crossed over"
     or "made her transition."
As Mom "made her transition
   to the other side,"
   those of us who stood at her grave
   missed her greatly
   but did not wish her back.

For my mother
   had *"fought the good fight"* (2 Timothy 4:7)
   of cancer, aging, and dementia,
   and now had *"won the race."*
A strong wind blew around us
   quite coincidently
   as we stood around her grave.
We all sensed in this
   her final message:

"No longer do I suffer here,
    wrapped in bodily weakness.
I have left this tomb behind!
Now I walk in the Light!"

"The other disciple outran Peter . . .
    and saw the wrappings
        on the ground.
He saw and believed" (John 20:4–8).

Too many people today
    walk through life
    caught up in the facades
        of earthly concerns.
Although technically still alive,
    they are already wrapped
    in burial cloths
        of darkness and death,
    or trapped in tombs
        of their own making.
"'Untie him,' Jesus told them,
    'and let him go free!'" (John 11:44)

Indeed, mere earthly issues do have a way
    of wrapping us in their grip
    and holding us bound.
We obsess daily
    about self-important human concerns,
    only to forget what they even were
        a month later.
Some travelers in this world
    even get trapped in
    "stinkin' thinkin'"—
    truly unhealthy patterns of
    compulsive neediness,
    obsessive fearfulness,
    depressive negativity.

But everyone born into time
    cannot help but occasionally feel "trapped"
    by this limited human condition—
    its struggles and uncertainties,
    its frustratingly close encounters
        with True Happiness.

But today we get the "big picture."
Easter is our "reality check,"
    reminding us
    of the Reality of Resurrection
        in the face of
    the tombs of this world!
"Death is swallowed up in victory.
O death, where is your victory?" (1 Corinthians 15:55)
At the dawn of Easter,
    this world's fears are obliterated
    and human preoccupations vanish
        in the flash of eternity's Light.
"'Untie him,' Jesus told them,
    'and let him go free!'"

Today, our great and mighty God,
    whose Power tore apart
        the wrappings of death,
        the traps of this earth,
    has a message for you.
"The law of the Spirit
    has freed you
    from the law of sin and death" (Romans 8:2).

Leave your tombs behind!
Walk in the healing Light
    that eternal Life sheds
    upon this world's facades.
Roll away those heavy stones
    from the tombs of your minds.

Free yourself from the traps
   imposed by the fears,
     worries,
      preoccupations,
   this earth imposes upon you.
Come forth into the Light
   of eternal Hope
   and soul-soothing Peace.
"I will give you a new heart,
   and place a new spirit
     within you" (Ezekiel 36:26).

Embrace this Fire in the Deep,
   this new Strength
     for your weary old life.
Walk confidently in the brightness
   of a new day
     every day—
   a day your God
     has given you!
Take hold of this Power for Living,
   that springs up
   even in the very face
   of death itself!
Seize that sweet, sweet Spirit
   that energizes,
     empowers,
     emboldens you to live!

Power for the Powerless

Second Sunday of Easter

(Acts 2:42–47; John 20:19–31)

Power.
The word means
   many things.
Electric power
   made this world modern.
Horsepower
   drives our cars.
Political power
   changes the communities
   we live in.
Physical power
   motivates athletes
   to great accomplishments.

Yet, despite all this power,
   why do so many feel utterly
    power-less in life?
People struggling with cancer
   or some terminal sickness
   feel little sense of control
    over their situation.

America's perpetual underprivileged
   have less "power-full" options
     available to them.
Even most faithful churchgoers
   seem to have little clue
     of the true Power
   lying within their rituals.

"I come that you might have life,
   and have it to the full" (John 10:10).
God is all about
   empowering the powerless.
The Deity whose creative Power
   brought Life to the universe,
   who shaped the sun,
     formed the forests,
   has unleashed an awesome Power
     upon this world.
It is a Power that can
   transform the underprivileged,
   motivate the mediocre,
     humble the proud.
That Power was released
   with four simple words:
   "Peace be with you!" (John 20:21)

That awesome gift of divine Peace
   in the midst of our human turmoil
     was like an oasis
   in the midst of desert sands.
When human life becomes ordered
   according to Peace's priorities
     (not human desires or lusts),
   an amazing inner calmness
   comes over the human soul.
People can accomplish
   truly unbelievable things.

"They shared all things in common;
they would sell property and goods,
dividing everything
on the basis of one's need" (Acts 2:44–45).

But the awesome Power of Peace
unleashed by the Spirit
is far from being mere
passive docility;
rather, it is an active Energy,
a dynamic Force
transforming everything
in its path.
It is Fire in the Deep.
"I have come to light a fire on the earth,
and how I wish it were kindled!" (Luke 12:49)

Some are healed physically
and emotionally
by Peace.
Others have their entire lifestyle
turned upside down.
Previously lukewarm people,
mired in mediocrity,
suddenly stand up boldly
for Truth.
People acquire true inner Power,
transforming the powers that be.

"Receive the Holy Spirit!" (John 20:22)
Jesus says to his followers.
With these words the Prince of Peace
empowers the powerless
to stand and speak boldly.
With these words, Emmanuel
emboldens the fearful
and embraces the lonely.

With these words,
    that Fire in the Deep
    begins its blazing path
        of personal transformation.

Receive the Peace
    that God offers to you this day.
Open your heart and mind
    to that Power-full Peace
        passing human understanding.

You will not be able
    to contain or control It.
You can only yield to It.
It will be a fiery Peace
    that affirms and empowers,
        even as It
    transforms and upends.
But you have nothing to fear—
    except your fear.

"Peace I leave with you;
    my peace I give to you.
Not as the world gives
    do I give it to you" (John 14:27).

Their Eyes Were Opened

Third Sunday of Easter

(Acts 2:14, 22–28; Luke 24:13–35)

A man was sentenced to death
   and placed in a dark cave
   with food for thirty days.
Told there was only one way out,
   he focused on a small hole
   in the roof above.
But despite building a mound
   and leaping up continuously,
   the man couldn't escape.
When the man's lifeless body was later removed,
   the light from the doorway
   revealed a hole in the wall
   opposite his mound.
So narrowly focused
   on the hole in the roof,
   the man missed
     the freedom
   hidden in the darkness.

How many of us
   have the same trouble
      seeing truth
      in our lives?
We get so preoccupied,
   so narrowly focused
      on our problems,
      worries,
      burdens,
   that we, too, are blind
   to wisdom and truth
      hidden plainly
      before us.
"They asked him
   'Lord, open our eyes!'" (Matthew 20:33)

Two thousand years ago,
   only days after Jesus' death,
   two men walked the dusty road
      out of Jerusalem,
   grieving the death
      of their Master.
So preoccupied with grief,
   so caught up in their loss,
   they blindly missed
      seeing the Truth
   suddenly appear in front of them!
"They were restrained
   from recognizing him" (Luke 24:16).

It was only as they
   walked with the Stranger,
   sharing their grief and loss,
      their disillusioned faith,
      their simmering hopes,
   that their blindness
      began to lift.

When finally the Stranger
  "took bread, broke it
  and distributed it to them" (Luke 24:30),
  Truth was suddenly revealed
  and darkness vanished.

It is the same with us.
Often it takes a while
  for our preoccupations,
    obsessions,
    blindness,
  to be openly revealed
  for what they are.
It is only when we, too,
  spend time walking with
    that mysterious "Stranger,"
    that "Truth-bringer,"
  slowly breathing in his peace,
  receiving that subtle
    Spirit-Wisdom,
  that our own *"eyes are opened."*

Only when we ourselves
  "break bread together" with Jesus—
  sharing daily the nourishment
    of God's Presence,
  taking faithfully into ourselves
    Life beyond life,
  that lifelong preoccupations,
    personality quirks,
    lingering denials,
  can finally be shed.
"You have shown me the paths of life;
  you will fill me with joy
    in your presence" (Acts 2:28).

Examine your life today
  for areas where divine Truth
  needs to break through
    human blindness.
Where might you be obsessing
  about misleading "holes in the roof,"
    while missing
  "doors hidden in darkness"?
Where might you be
  walking in blindness,
  caught up in fear and worry,
  while Freedom and Light
    are staring you
    in the face?
Where are you walking
  that dusty road
  of preoccupation
    and ignorance,
  while Truth walks
    at your side
    all the while?

Remember this day to
  "walk by faith,
    not by sight" (2 Corinthians 5:7).
Do not *"be concerned*
  about many things,
  when only one thing
    is necessary" (Luke 10:41).
Open your eyes to Truth!
Walk with the Stranger named Jesus,
  drink deeply of his Wisdom,
  and allow your own eyes
    to be opened!

The Shepherd's Prayer

Fourth Sunday of Easter

(Psalm 23)

"The Lord is my shepherd . . . " (Psalm 23:1).
Precious Lord,
   my whole identity,
   my entire purpose
     and destiny in life,
   is caught up with you.
You are my beginning and end.
All that I have,
   or ever hope to be,
   I owe it all to you.
My entire being
   is wrapped up in you.
I am leaning on your
   everlasting arms.

". . . there is nothing I shall want."
Good and Gracious God,
   my humanity wants much
     from this world,
   but all I truly need
     comes from you.

Help me to see
    what is of lasting, eternal value
    in this passing world.
Free me from obsessing
    about selfish desires
      or petty problems
    that pass away as quickly
      as the night.

"In green pastures you give me repose" (Psalm 23:2).
My Faithful Friend,
    your ways always lead me
      eventually but inevitably
    to that quiet place
      where peace passes understanding.
A single moment with you
    in your green pastures
      is worth more
    than a thousand elsewhere
      of fame, power, or wealth.
Help me to seek peace
    in my own soul this day.

"He refreshes my soul" (Psalm 23:3).
Master and Teacher,
    my soul is tired—
    tired from searching,
      struggling,
      surviving
    in this frenetic, troubled world.
But when I come to you,
    I find the refreshment
    my thirsty soul yearns for.
I gain more by resting quietly
    against and in you,
      than I do
    by all my restless efforts
      elsewhere.

You are the Waters that refresh,
   the Life that nourishes,
   the Mercy that heals.

"Even though I walk
   through a dark valley . . . " (Psalm 23:4).
My wounded Healer,
   by your cross and Resurrection,
     You set us free.
Why do I so easily forget
   that even you were not spared
     from suffering?
Why do I think that I
   somehow should be exempt from pain,
     spared from sorrow,
     freed from grief?
Help me not so much to
   avoid life's "dark valleys,"
   grumble about them,
   become a "martyr" over them,
     but to simply
keep my eyes fixed on you
     in the midst of them.
After all, you are my Rock,
   my Fortress,
     my True Deliverer.

"I will fear no evil,
   for You are at my side."
My Healer and Redeemer,
   why should I feel discouraged,
   why should the shadows fall?
Why should my heart be lonely,
   and long for heaven above?
Your "eye is on the sparrow,"
   and I know you watch over me.

When darkness comes round about me,
   I have nothing to fear,
   for your *"rod and staff*
     give me courage" (Psalm 23:4).
Your last words on earth
   are ever etched in my soul:
   "I am with you always,
   until the end of time" (Matthew 28:20).

"'I will dwell in the house of the Lord
   for years to come" (Psalm 23:6).
My Brother and Guide,
   you are my Final Destination,
     my Goal,
     my Purpose
   and my Reason for Living.
In you I live
   and move
   and have my very being.
Your Goodness and Love
   pursue me
   all the days
     of my life.
Use me while I am here,
   but take me Home,
     where I belong,
   when life's little journey
     is complete.

Amen, my Lord!
Amen, my Shepherd!
Amen, my Dear Friend!

Our Secret Identity

Fifth Sunday of Easter

(1 Peter 2:4–9; John 14:1–12)

Every true "superhero"
  in comic books and TV
  has a secret identity.
Generations of people
  grew up on the words:
    "And who, disguised as
    a mild-mannered reporter
    named Clark Kent . . . "
Superman, Batman, Power Rangers—
  all hid their real identity
  behind a false front and name.

In our modern world,
  many of us may feel
  like we, too, have
    "split identities."
We are one person
  in school,
  in the work world,
  in our "professional life,"
    and yet another

around our friends,
   our intimates.
Indeed, this is needed.
But if we cannot separate
   these often conflicting
      parts of life,
   problems can ensue.

Despite the masks we don
   to the world,
     and even with intimates,
       sometimes
   our deepest identity
   is hidden even
     from ourselves.
So many people today
   do not really know
     themselves.
So many people
   give scarcely a thought
   to the deep Truth
     of their own *true* identity,
   the singularity of their soul
     in the Creator's plan.

"O Lord, you have probed me,
   and you know me.
With all my ways
   you are familiar" (Psalm 139:1–3).
Who we are with regard to our jobs and friends—
   who we have become
     in this world—
   is not who we truly are
     with God.
Contrary to what many believe,
   we *are* not our jobs
     or the money we make
     or the power we have.

We *are* not personally defined
   by our children,
      our accomplishments,
      or our failures.

We all have a secret identity
   beyond this world,
   and it is this:
"You are a chosen race,
   a royal priesthood,
   a holy nation,
   a people God claims
      for his own" (1 Peter 2:9).
Your secret identity
   is that you are valued by God—
   valued for who you are,
      not
   what you do, create, or produce.
Your being has an infinite dignity,
   and incomparable beauty
   no one can take from you!

"Because you are precious
   in my eyes and glorious,
   because I love you!" (Isaiah 43:4)
Your life has meaning,
   has a purpose and destiny
      beyond anything
   this world can do to you!
Knowing your true identity,
   and returning to its Truth
      daily,
   is the single greatest key
   to calming your restless spirit,
   and surviving the challenges of life.

Reflect this day on
   your true inner identity!

Know well who you truly are,
    from where you come,
    to where you are bound.
What you become each day
    is an illusion—
    but who you are
       is Truth.
Remind yourself each morning
    of this great Truth:
    you have a name
       that only God knows.
Keep in mind this powerful life-secret
    as you walk daily
       through life's illusions:
"Do not let your heart be troubled" (John 14:1).
Know that your God
    is with you always,
       and that
    you need fear nothing
       in this world
       or from this world.
Your identity is firm,
    your worth is eternal.
Rejoice in who you are—
    and Whose you are!

Sixth Sunday of Easter

(1 Peter 3:15–18; John 14:15–21)

"I will not leave you orphaned" (John 14:18).
A friend tells a childhood story
   of being left behind
   at a park while on a trip
    with her parents.
Although scared and lonely,
   she wisely remained
   in the same location
   until her parents returned
    to pick her up.
But she has never forgotten
   the fear she felt
    at that moment.

There is in this life
   no greater personal fear
   than that of being forgotten,
    ignored,
    or abandoned.
And there probably is
   no greater contemporary crisis
   in this modern world

than the massive abandonments
occurring everywhere.

Child-victims of war,
the oft-forgotten casualties
of "easy divorce."
Seniors in nursing homes,
unvisited and often neglected.
Adults living lonely lives
of solitude and isolation.
"Orphans" are, indeed,
found everywhere today.

One of the greatest marks
of true friendship
is that a friend
is always there for us.
Sometimes by well-chosen words
or by their simple presence,
perhaps
by silent but powerful actions—
true friends keep people
from feeling "orphaned."
Their presence and faithfulness
are anchors amidst
the uncertain seas of life.

But if human companionship
and personal presence
reassures and calms,
how immensely more powerful it is
to know that God
"is with us until the end of time" (Matthew 28:20).
How soul-soothing it is
to simply sit
in the eternal Presence
of your Best Friend—

the Creator God who says,
"I have carved you
on the palm of my hand" (Isaiah 49:16).

How comforting are those words
    spoken by the Son of God
        some two thousand years ago—
"I will ask my Father,
and he will give you
    a Paraclete ["defender"]
to be with you always" (John 14:16).
How peace-filling to hear
    the quiet words of Jesus:
    "I will not leave you orphaned."

Whatever the stress in your life,
    the problems with family
        or friends,
    the tensions from job
        or finances—
    be reassured now
        that your God
        is always present.
Recall that the Name
    of our divine Deity
        is "Emmanuel"—
meaning *"God with us."*
In this uncertain universe,
    be anchored in the certainty
        of the *"Paraclete"*
who is always with you.

Then, rooted in this Truth,
    go out of your Self
    to touch some of those
        "orphaned"
        by this world.

Move beyond your own pains
 to ease the abandonment
  so many feel daily.
Take the Love within you,
 and give it to lonely souls,
  to abandoned children,
  to bone-weary seniors,
  to stressed single parents.
Speak to others the words
 your God has spoken to you:
 "I do not leave you orphaned;
 I will come back to you" (John 14:18).

In God's Kingdom,
 there are no orphans.
Receive this Truth
 in your own life.
Give away this Truth
 to others' lives.
In these two actions,
 salvation lies.

When Dreams Are Tossed and Torn

Seventh Sunday of Easter

(1 Peter 4:13–16; John 17:1–11)

"I know well the plans
I have for you" (Jeremiah 29:11).
Two young black men grew up
    in inner-city Chicago.
One became a gang member,
    killing his grandmother
        at the age of twelve;
    and was killed, in turn,
        by his own gang.
The other left the streets,
    received a Ph.D.,
    and now manages
        a mental-health facility.
Two similar men,
    two similar backgrounds,
    two very different dreams.

Every person born into time
    is born with an inner Dream
        placed there by God.

This Dream is composed of
   hopes and skills,
   dignity and beauty,
   potentials and possibilities.
But unfortunately in today's world
   things happen to Dreams.

Some Dreams get stolen
   by bad influences or people.
Others get gradually abandoned
   as poor choices eat them away.
Some slowly fade into fantasy
   as harsh reality
   drowns one's spirits
      again and again.

It is an evil thing
   when one's Dream is stolen—
   but luckily we have
      a Dream-Restorer!
It is part of the Divine Plan
   for this world
      to restore lost Dreams.
Indeed, God is the Ultimate Dreamer—
   finding hope even in failure,
      bringing life even in death.
When a person's life-dreams,
   their goals, hopes, and plans,
      get shattered or torn,
   God reveals his unique
      "Dream Renewal Plan."
"Know well the plans I have for you—
   plans for your welfare
   and not for your woe" (Jeremiah 29:11).

The first step in this Plan
 is to move your Self
 into even more intimate contact
  with the Original Dreamer.
Re-orient your life-view
 to embrace the Fire
 of the one Friend
 who never abandons you.
Remind yourself that your greatest dream
 is an eternal Dream.
"Eternal life is this:
 to know you,
  the only true God" (John 17:3).

If you have a hard time
 believing in life or love,
 seeing any goodness at all,
  know that the Original Dreamer
 has not stopped believing in you.
Your Dreams are God's Dreams.
Indeed, God prays for you:
"For these I pray—
 not for the world
 but for those you have given me,
 for they are really yours" (John 17:9).

A second step is to always vision
 New Dreams for your life.
Dreams, plans, and hopes
 are meant to change
 as Life reshapes life.
New Dreams may look different,
 happen in different places,
 be energized by different people.
The Dreams God plants in a soul
 may get amended and altered—
  but they never die.

Take time away by yourself
    to search the depths
        of your spirit.
Sit quietly with your Friend,
    allow that "Fire in the Deep"
        to rekindle your fires.
From the ashes of the old
    will come the embers of the new—
        New Dreams for Self,
        New Directions for Life.
"Rejoice insofar as you
    share Christ's suffering.
For then God's spirit
    has come to rest on you" (1 Peter 4:13).

Lastly, never walk alone
    when your personal Dreams
        get shattered.
Spend time with others
    who can support and love you.
True friends nourish the spirit,
    and renew your Dreams.
"They went to the upstairs room . . .
    together they devoted themselves
        to constant prayer" (Acts 1:13–14).

The Uncontrollable One

Pentecost

(Acts 2:1–11; John 20:19–23)

"Then he breathed on them and said,
  'Receive the Holy Spirit'" (John 20:22).
Jeremiah was thrown
   down a dry well.
John the Baptist hid out
   in the desert.
Francis Assisi was rejected
   by his own father,
      and met resistance from within
   the very group he founded.
Martin Luther wanted only reform,
   but ended beginning something new.
Pope John XXIII wanted only
   adaptation and renewal,
   but got anger and resistance.

Through all of history,
   people have been afraid
   of the Holy Spirit,
   of the charismatic Fire
      that is our God.

When prophetic people speak
   of the Spirit of God,
   the results are often
      fear,
      hesitation,
      even anger.
After infuriating the Jews
   with a Sabbath healing,
     Jesus told them,
"I came into this world
*   to make the blind see*
*   and the seeing blind"* (John 9:39).

In a world truly fixated
   on control and predictability,
   the Fire of God's Spirit
   is elusive and surprising,
     freeing and energizing.
One simply cannot control Fire!
The Spirit will always move
   in unexpected directions—
     opening unseen doors,
     upsetting preconceptions,
   breathing Life into stale routine,
   shocking with starkly simple Truth.
Richard Rohr says it well:
   "People fear this part of God
     that we cannot control
     or explain or merit;
   which is seductive,
     cannot be legislated,
     measured,
     mandated.
We do not like this part of God
   which is dove, water,
     and invisible wind"
     (*Everything Belongs*, Crossroad, 1999).

———

"Suddenly from up in the sky
  there came a noise
    like a strong, driving wind.
All were filled with the Holy Spirit.
They began to express themselves
  in foreign tongues" (Acts 2:2).
When the Fire of God flames up,
  it may seem a "foreign language"
  to those attempting to understand
    the event or message.
Far too many crave safety and security
  over the exhilarating Freedom
    of Good News!
But while many prefer to remain
  behind locked doors in fear,
  barricaded behind legislation,
  God's Spirit always moves ahead,
    bringing gospel freedom,
    prophetic truth,
    spiritual renewal.
One simply cannot control Fire!

"Receive the Holy Spirit!" (John 20:22)
Remain open to the charismatic,
  to the uncontrollable Fire
    that is God burning in the Deep.
Do not allow encrusted attitudes
  or habitual religious ritual
    to blind you
  to Power-full new ways of living,
    praying, and acting.
Dare to venture beyond
  carefully controlled certitudes
    and predictable platitudes.

Risk being enflamed by the Spirit
   of Truth and Love;
   then rise up to serve
   in the Spirit
     of Courage and Trust.

"The wind blows where it will.
You hear the sound it makes
   but you don't know where it comes from,
     or where it goes.
So it is with everyone
   born of the Spirit" (John 3:8).
Allow God's Spirit to blow freely
   through your spirit,
   upsetting preconceptions,
   reordering your house.
Put yourself into places
   that move you into the Power
     of Spirit-led convictions.
Be with people who empower you
   to say, "Jesus is Lord!"

This is Pentecost!
This is Jesus
   saying to fearful people,
   "Peace be with you!" (John 20:21)
This is the Fire of God
   moving in the Deep Places—
     beyond logic and control.
This is the Spirit of God saying,
   "Receive the Holy Spirit!" (John 20:23)

Conjunctio Oppositorum

Trinity Sunday

(Exodus 34:4–9; Daniel 3:52–56; John 3:16–18)

Conjunctio oppositorum.
This Latin phrase,
   used by Carl Jung,
    means the "union of opposites."
It refers to seemingly
   contradictory forces
    merging together
   to form a new entity.
Chemicals hydrogen and oxygen
   combine to form water,
    for example.
Two very unique people
   join together in marriage—
   and despite their differences,
   their union becomes a sacrament
    of life and love.

Truly the God of our universe
   is *conjunctio oppositorum.*
Like no other force in the world,
    our Supreme Being brings together
   images that seem
    utterly incompatible.
The very Essence of Divinity,
   is uncreated Nature,
   and is therefore innately
     paradoxical,
     enigmatic,
     contradictory,
     mysterious.
"As afar as the heavens
   are above the earth,
    so great is his love" (Psalm 103:11).
The paradoxes of Divine Power
   truly stretch and strain
   our simple human minds.

Our God is *"holy and glorious,*
   praiseworthy and exalted
   above all forever" (Daniel 3:53),
     yet to humanity
     God is also
   "merciful and gracious,
    slow to anger,
    rich in kindness" (Exodus 34:8).
God gazes upon the eternal ages
   "from his throne
    upon the cherubim" (Daniel 3:56),
    yet God's concern for each person
    is such that
  "every hair of your head
   is numbered" (Matthew 10:30).

From one perspective,
   God *"alone is to be feared,*
   from heaven he has pronounced
     judgment" (Psalm 76:7–8),
   yet *"God so loved the world*
     that he gave his only Son" (John 3:16).
At these awesome realizations,
   all any human mind can say is
     "Praise be the name of God!"

But going even further,
   God is *conjunctio oppositorum*
   for anyone who becomes
   a serious believer.
In other words, this God for whom
   "a thousand years are as a day" (2 Peter 3:8)
   will turn life upside down
   when he moves into
     your deepest places!

Certainly the foundation
   of the divine-human relationship
   is that God loves and cherishes us.
"You are precious in my eyes,
   and I love you" (Isaiah 43:4).
Yet, Divine Love is also "tough Love,"
   pushing us beyond our Self—
   prodding us to grow and change,
     to move far beyond
     mere ritual faithfulness.
If you follow God long enough,
   you will inevitably be "stretched"
   far beyond your comfort zones—
   because God loves you enough
   not to leave you
     where you are!

Open your mind to take in
　　the breadth and length
　　of the God who is
　　　　conjunctio oppositorum.
Let your spirit be stretched
　　by the One who is both
　　"water of life"
　　　　and *"fire of the Spirit."*
Allow your Self to be pushed
　　beyond human comprehension
　　into the depth
　　　　of Divine Mystery.

You will be healed by Mercy,
　　and yet fractured by Grace.
You will be energized by Life,
　　and challenged by Truth.
You will be awed by Creation's magnificence,
　　and yet humbled by Love.

You will arrive at a Place
　　of utter simplicity,
　　　　a quiet Center,
　　where all that can be said is
　　　　I am.
　　　　God is.
　　　　Grace flows.
　　　　That is enough!
Your only response
　　to this awesome God
　　will be that of Moses—
*"Bow down to the ground
　　in worship"* (Exodus 34:8).

Nutritious and Delicious

Corpus Christi

(Deuteronomy 8:2–3, 14–16; John 6:51–58)

"Taste and see
  how good the Lord is" (Psalm 34:9).
At a museum recently,
  I toured one exhibit
  dedicated to nutrition and food.
There were exhibits
  on food packaging,
    nutritional value,
    how food is grown,
    and more.
I left very conscious
  of the central role
    food plays in life.

Of all the things
  humans do daily,
    few are more important
      than eating.

Food is not only
   nourishment and strength,
   it is also symbolic—
     of friendship,
     fellowship,
     hospitality.
Thus it is not surprising
   that food was important
     to God, too.
Throughout human history,
   our Supreme Being uses food
   to remind us of his Presence.

"The Lord . . . gave you manna
   to eat in the desert" (Deuteronomy 8:16).
Moses and the Israelites
   were told to eat
   a final "pass-over" meal
   before their exodus
     from Egypt's slavery.
The prophet Elisha
   multiplied bread
     in 2 Kings 4,
   anticipating by a century
     what Jesus would do.
Jesus Christ often shared meals
   with close friends
   or others he sought to touch.

But the Son of God
   knew there was one problem
     with any human food—
   it only satisfies temporarily.
People continue to get
   hungry and thirsty,
   always having to eat again;
   and despite our eating,
     we still die.

Earthly nourishment
   simply cannot satisfy
      the human spirit.
We need eternal food,
   nourishment that fills
      our deepest hungers,
         and sates our private thirsts.

Thus Jesus said to us,
"I am the living bread
   come down from heaven.
If anyone eats of this bread,
   they will live forever" (John 6:51).
Jesus gave us himself
   as the Food of eternal Life,
   telling us to literally
      take him
      into our Self.
"Take this and eat it,
   this is my body" (Matthew 26:26).

When we receive Eucharist,
   it is a passport to new Life.
"Whoever eats my flesh
   and drinks my blood
      has eternal life" (John 6:54).

When we take Jesus into our Self,
   we receive the Seed-promise
   of full body-healing.
"Lord, I am not worthy
   that you should come . . .
   only say the word
      and I shall be healed."

When we sit down at table
   to Commune with other believers,
   we truly become One.

There are no differences
   of color, race, or politics.
"Because there is one loaf,
   we who are many are one body,
   for we all partake
     of the one loaf" (1 Corinthians 10:17).

The Food that Jesus gives us
   is eternal Nourishment—
   satisfying the deepest hungers
     of the human heart,
   sating our searching spirits.
"Whoever drinks the water I give
   will never be thirsty" (John 4:14).

Know and appreciate well
   the miracle occurring
     when you receive God's Food.
Partake in the Eucharist
   with a deep sense
     of expectant Power.
Celebrate with praise
   what Jesus does
   as he feeds your soul
     with Life eternal!
Receive your Master
   with joy and anticipation!
"Taste and see
   how good the Lord is" (Psalm 34:8).

Harvesting for the Lord

Eleventh Sunday in Ordinary Time

(Exodus 19:2–6; Matthew 9:36–10:8)

"The harvest is good
 but the laborers are few" (Matthew 9:37).
If Jesus walked the world today,
  he would easily repeat
    these same words.
Millions of people
  search for a purpose in life.
Myriad injustices
  cry out for a voice.
This modern world
  is far from the vision of unity
    Jesus preached.

Indeed, the *"harvest"*
  of Godly work to be done
    is huge.
There is no shortage of places
  that need Good News today,
  or of people who yearn for
    the Touch that heals,
    the Word that calms,
    the Look that soothes.

"They were lying prostrate
  from exhaustion,
    like sheep without a shepherd" (Matthew 9:36).

What there is a shortage of
  is laborers willing to work
  in this vast vineyard
    of lost souls
    and searching spirits.
Jesus Christ needs men and women
  who will help with the harvest—
  people who will be
    full-time apostles for God,
  not merely part-time disciples.
Will you be one of those who
  "helps with the harvest"?
"Beg the harvest-master to send out
  laborers to gather his harvest" (Matthew 9:38).

There are many reasons *not*
  to work for the Lord.
Godly work is frequently frustrating,
  the response discouraging.
The hours are lonely and long,
  the allurements of this world
    strong and pervasive.

But I give personal witness
  that the blessings
    of working for the Lord
  far outweigh any burdens!
What you give to others
  always comes back to you
    multiplied and increased!
"Give, and it will be given back to you.
Good measure, flowing over,
  will they pour
    into the folds of your garment" (Luke 6:38).

First, harvesting for the Lord
   brings a Peace this world
      can never give.
Becoming a full-time apostle
   pulls you into the deep calmness
   of a love relationship with Divinity
      unmatched
   by anything this world has to offer.
As you go out daily to work
   in the "fields of harvest,"
   you *will* hear God say,
"I bear you up on eagle's wings,
   and bring you here to myself.
You are my special possession,
   dearer to me than all other people" (Exodus 19:4–5).

Second, you will have gifts from God,
   and support from the people
      harvesting with you.
Before Jesus sent out his apostles,
   "he gave them authority
   to expel unclean spirits,
   cure sickness and diseases
      of every kind" (Matthew 10:1).
These gifts of God's Spirit
   are still very real today,
   still very available today
      for those who believe.
You will never be lonely
   on your "harvest journey"—
   companions will mysteriously
      be there
   just when you need them.

Lastly, the "harvest hours"
  of God's work in this world
    may be long,
  but God's retirement plan
    is truly "out of this world"!
When you work full-time for the Lord,
  you will indeed get tired,
    worn out,
    beaten down,
    frustrated,
    even discouraged.
But you will have eternity to rest!
The benefits of working for the Lord
  are truly fantastic:
  forgiveness of all sins,
  compassion enough to heal
    your deepest hurts,
  fellowship forever
    with family and friends,
  the fullness of joy
    and eternal happiness,
  Life forever with the Almighty!

"Go to the lost sheep
  of the house of Israel.
Make this announcement:
  'The reign of God
    is at hand!'" (Matthew 10:6–7)

Fatherhood

Twelfth Sunday in Ordinary Time

(Jeremiah 20:10–13; Matthew 10:26–33)

*"A wise son heeds
    his father's instructions"* (Proverbs 13:1).
A recent English poll
    reveals the "most admired" persons
    to be mothers.
Fathers were fifth on the list,
    following even the queen.
For years now television shows
    have highlighted father figures
    who are bumbling and incompetent.
Now, with artificial insemination,
    some claim fathers
        are completely unnecessary.

Sadly, the value of fatherhood
    has greatly diminished
    in our modern world.
Certainly there are problems
    with men today—
        lack of commitment,
        rising single parenthood,
        uncertain male identity.

All these are true and valid.
But demeaning the value of fatherhood,
    and its role in culture,
    is a road to ruin
        for any society.

God thought enough of fatherhood
    to make it the foundation
    of the relationship between
    the Word made Flesh Jesus
        and the Creator God.
Jesus had an intimate relationship
    with his Father,
    often turning to him
        in times of trouble.
It was a relationship of strength,
    trust and honesty,
    confidence and security.
"The Lord is with me,
    like a mighty champion" (Jeremiah 20:11).

Jesus taught his own disciples
    to honor the Father and
    to *"praise the Lord,*
  for he has rescued
    the life of the poor
  from the power
    of the wicked" (Jeremiah 20:13).
Three times in today's Gospel,
    Jesus speaks of his own
        "Father in heaven."

Reflect today on your own father—
    both your earthly father,
    and your heavenly Father.

If your own father was not perfect,
    was not there for you,
    was flawed or broken—
    allow the Father of Jesus
        to make up
        for what is lacking.
Reform your image of "father"
    to conform to the image
    Jesus Christ has
        of his Father.

First, Jesus called his Father *Abba*—
    the Aramaic word for "Daddy."
The Father of the God-Man Jesus
    is One who can always
        be relied upon,
        be trusted totally,
        be loving
    in both gentle ways
    and tough ways
        if needed.
"Do not be afraid of anything,
    you are worth more
    than a flock of sparrows" (Matthew 10:31).

Second, the Father of Jesus
    has wisdom, knowledge, and strength
        for all your needs.
Turn to this Father
    for the direction you seek
    and the answers you need
        in your life journey.
The Spirit of your heavenly Father
    will always be there
    to guide, support, and empower.

"The words I speak
are not spoken of myself;
it is my Father within me
accomplishing his works" (John 14:10).

Lastly, the Father of Jesus
    is totally unselfish
    and completely generous.
Think for a moment—
    what else
    could the Author of your life
        do for you?
The Father-Creator birthed your being,
    put latent gifts deep within,
    gave friendship and love,
    sent Jesus when we were in sin,
    empowers us with Spirit
        when we are weak.

Total trust, deep wisdom,
    complete unselfishness—
    truly this is the Fatherhood
    our world and being longs for.

Commit yourself to promote
    strong yet gentle images
    of fathers in the world today.
Examine your own relationship
    with God the Father.
Talk to the Father daily.
Let his unshakeable love heal you.
Put your hand in his hand,
    and allow him to lead you
    to his home in paradise!

Going All the Way

Thirteenth Sunday in Ordinary Time

(2 Kings 4:8–16; Matthew 10:37–42)

Here's a quiz for you.
   If your car starts
      two days out of three,
      is it "faithful"?
If your refrigerator
   quits working occasionally,
   would you say,
   "Well, it works
      most of the time"?
If you come to work
   two of every three days,
   would your boss consider you
      "committed"?
Few people would tolerate such things
   as signs of faithfulness.

But why is it that many
   can't seem to find daily time
      for God,
   yet consider themselves
      "faithful"?

Why is it that people
    wear expensive gold crosses,
    attend worship perhaps twice a year,
    yet breezily say,
        "I'm a faithful Christian."
Why is it that people say,
    "Yes, I love God,
        but
I'm not a fanatic about it!"

Today Jesus speaks his
    most challenging message of all.
"Whoever loves father or mother,
    son or daughter,
        more than me
    is not worthy of me" (Matthew 10:37).
This is not an attack on family life,
    but rather an insistence that
    following God is more important,
        more central
    than *any* other life-commitment
        or life-event.
There is no room here
    for half-hearted, wishy-washy,
        tentative commitment.
Either a person takes Jesus seriously
    in each and every area
        of life,
    or else *"he is not worthy of me."*

"Whoever finds his life will lose it,
    and whoever loses his life
        for my sake
        will find it" (Matthew 10:39).

These are truly radical, hard words.
Author E. Stanley Jones said it best:
  "Most people have been inoculated
  with a mild form of Christianity
  so they'll be immune
    to the real thing."
Many faithful church-attenders,
  many who profess to be believers,
  many "spiritual" people,
  have problems surrendering to God
    in this total fashion.
A faith-full commitment to God
  is a total *life*-commitment
    to God.
It calls for absolute allegiance
  to the values espoused
    by Jesus Christ.
It calls for the highest loyalty,
  disregarding any public consequences
    or familial ramifications.
It calls for wholehearted following
    in every area of one's life
  of the teachings,
    exhortations,
    wisdom,
    and Life of the Master.
"I wish that you would be hot or cold,
  but because you are lukewarm,
  I will spit you
    out of my mouth" (Revelation 3:15–16).

The God who shaped and created you
  has entered this world
    in human form.
The Almighty Being who formed you
  offers you eternal Life
    by imitating his life.

The "Highest Power" of the universe
    offers you a *"peace*
        the world cannot give" (John 14:27).
The task of following Jesus Christ,
    of taking seriously
        his words of Life,
    means going "all the way"
        with your God,
        with your life.

Christianity is not a spectator sport,
    not an add-on module to life,
    not a part-time job,
    not an insurance policy
        against eternal damnation.
Faith in God is a participatory experience,
    an attitude-transforming event,
    a full-time commitment,
    a life-changing phenomenon.

How far are you willing to go
      for the God who died for you?
How much of your life
    will you give the One
      who gave it all for you?
Will you go all the way
    for your God?

WEEK 35

God of Contradictions

Fourteenth Sunday in Ordinary Time

(Zechariah 9:9–10; Matthew 11:25–30)

"Take my yoke
upon your shoulders
and learn from me" (Matthew 11:29).
Few today know what a yoke is—
   a harness covering
   the shoulders of oxen,
     linking them
   to a plow or cart.

When Jesus tells us to
   "take my yoke"
   on our shoulders,
     it seems absurd.
By instinct, the human spirit
   rebels against
     such an enslaving encumbrance
     used by animals.
It denotes slavery
   and personal restraint—
   two highly "un-American" concepts.
Yet there is deep spiritual wisdom
   in this well-chosen image.

Our God is a "God of Contradictions."
Our God rarely acts as we expect,
   and frequently uses
      illogical incongruities
   to teach eternal Truths.
Our "God of Contradictions"
   uses simple yet profound images
   to disturb our comfortableness,
   to provoke our thinking,
   to challenge our complacency,
   to teach profound Wisdom.

Taking on the "yoke"
   of Jesus' teaching
   (for example)
   may seem to be a heavy load—
      restrictive,
      burdensome,
      stifling.
Yet, in reality,
   only in Jesus Christ
   does one find true Life,
      inner Freedom,
      soul-soothing Peace,
      eternal Redemption.
Thus the apparent "burden"
   of faith and religion,
   of personal spiritual discipline,
      becomes light and easy,
   as our spirit finds true Freedom
   from the "yokes" of this world's
      enslaving forces.

"What you have hidden
   from the learned and clever,
   you have revealed
   to the merest of children" (Matthew 11:25).

Yet another startling contrast:
   mere children learn
   what wise sages fail to see?
It seems absurd!
But again our "God of Contradictions"
   speaks deep wisdom
     to this world.
It takes a childlike simplicity,
   youthful openness and trust,
   to perceive the heart
     of divine Truth.
The accumulated "wisdom,"
   the common sense and logic
     of adulthood,
   is utterly useless.
In what area of *your* life
   do you need to learn
     this profound lesson?

"See, your king shall come to you . . .
   meek and riding on an ass" (Zechariah 9:9).
A king riding an ass?
The mind boggles
   at this laughable image.
Yet, our "God of Contradictions"
   chose this humble transport
     to enter into Jerusalem
   and to perfectly symbolize
     his own Nature and Message.

Do not be fooled
   by external appearances
   or the fronts, fakes, and facades
     of this world.
The things of greatest value
   (spirituality, Truth, Love)
   are mostly disguised
     in common cloaks.

———

Keep your eyes open
    as you read Scripture
    and walk through this world.
Seek for and learn to read
    the often paradoxical Wisdom
       of our "God of Contradictions."
Incongruous imagery,
    strange coincidences,
    apparent illogic,
    often reveal deep Divine Truth.

A divine Being named Word
    created us all,
       yet
    a human Being born a baby
      saved us all!
The Lord of the Universe judges,
    yet the Prince of Peace saves!
Praise be to our amazing
    "God of Contractions,"
    "whose thoughts
      are not your thoughts" (Isaiah 55:8),
    and whose mysterious Wisdom
    will change your life,
    and transform your spirit!

Inevitability

Fifteenth Sunday in Ordinary Time

(Isaiah 55:10–11; Romans 8:18–23; Matthew 13:1–23)

> *"My word that goes forth*
>   *from my mouth*
>   *shall not return to me void"* (Isaiah 55:11).
> The old saying is that there are
>   two inevitable things in life:
>   death and taxes.
> (According to recent research,
>   we may need to add
>   cockroaches to that list!)
> Some things in life
>   are truly unavoidable:
>   night always follows day;
>   human bodies are weakened
>   by age or disease;
>   all things mechanical
>   break down;
>   and "Murphy's Law" is real!

Some human occurrences as well
   seem unavoidable:
   the challenges of raising children,
   the difficult demands of a job
     or relationship,
   the presence of problems
     despite one's status or wealth.
As we face the inescapable inevitability
   of all things human and personal,
   it is a blessing to realize
   there is also inevitability
     about our God.

"Just as the rain and snow come down . . .
   so shall my word be . . .
   it will do my will,
   achieving the end
     for which I sent it" (Isaiah 55:10–11).
Just as winter follows fall,
   and rain falls on the earth,
   so God's words bear fruit,
   his Power finds purpose,
   his Promises are full-filled.

When God's *"word goes out"*—
   that is, when God "speaks a word,"
     makes a Promise,
     utters a Truth—
   its power and accomplishment
     are already guaranteed.
God's word is not empty or false.
The God who *is* Truth
   cannot speak insincerely
   or artificially
     as humans often do.
God's words have the Power
   to accomplish that which
     they promise!

God's words have the fiery
   inevitability of eternity
     behind them.

"One day a farmer went out sowing.
Part of the seed landed on good soil
   and yielded grain
   of a hundred- or sixty-
     or thirty-fold" (Matthew 13:4-8).
God is the Divine Farmer
   planting seeds
     of Promise and Hope
   through all time.
Planted quietly and simply,
   their Fruit inevitably bursts forth
   in unexpectedly different
     and varied degrees.
The seeds of God's Word
   find flower in the tender mercies
     and amazing graces
   which arise to surprise
     our weary spirits.

The "seeds" of Divine Promise
   will sprout within you—
   but the "soil" of your spirit
   determines the fullness
     of their flowering.
If your faith and hope
   lack the depth
     of true commitment,
   or is choked with thorns
     of false priorities,
   the seeds of Divine Power
   cannot bear fruit
     to their fullest.

Reflect today on the power,
   reliability,
   and inevitability
   of God's promises to you.
Then ponder carefully the preparedness,
   the receptiveness of the "soil"
   of your inner spirit
      and personal life-attitudes.

"I will be with you always
   until the end of time" (Matthew 28:20).
God has promised to be
   Present with Power
      in every life-struggle.
This is an inescapable *fact*,
   not a phony placebo
   to pacify people.
But can you receive this Truth,
   sit at peace within it,
   act with gentleness
      and justice
      because of it?

"Yes, we know that all creation groans,
   but the sufferings of the present
      are as nothing
   compared to the glory
      to be revealed in us" (Romans 8:18).
The Word has gone out.
The Seeds are planted.
Wait now
   with confident expectation.

Seeds of Justice

Sixteenth Sunday in Ordinary Time

(Romans 8:26–27; Matthew 13:24–43)

Young people shot down
   before their time.
Tragic air crashes
   and auto accidents.
Criminals seemingly getting away
   with their crimes.
At times, it seems quite justified
   that some cry out,
     "Where is God in all this?
     Where is justice and fairness?"

Indeed, perhaps the oldest,
   most asked questions
   of the eternal God
     have been,
     "Why do unjust things happen?
     Why does God not act in power
       at horrible times?
     Why do the heavens seem silent?"
At such times, one's body and spirit
   stand mute trying
     to comprehend it all.

The confusing illogic of the world
and our human condition
may seem overwhelming.

Thus, at first the story Jesus tells
may seem nonsensical.
"The reign of God is like a man
who sowed good seed in his field.
While everyone was asleep,
his enemy came and sowed weeds,
and then made off.
When the crop began to mature,
the weeds made their appearance
as well" (Matthew 13:24).
What do seeds and weeds
have to do with
injustice,
unfairness?
But there is power-full
and symbolic wisdom here.

The Good in this world
springing forth from God's touch
is inextricably mixed
with the Evil flowing from
an opposite Power.
The world around us is the field,
the "battleground"
where these two forces collide
throughout human history.
We should never expect absence
of the "weeds" of inequity and evil
as we ourselves struggle
to "grow the good seed"
of our own lives.
Never expect perfection
in this world.

Do not expect to always make sense
  of the nonsense of random evil
  and a broken human condition.

"Do you want us to pull them up?'
'No,' he replied, 'pull up the weeds
  and you might take the wheat
    along with them.
Let them grow together until harvest'"
  (Matthew 13:29–30).
As humans with limited insight,
  we are unable to see
  the mysterious myriad ways
  Divine Power moves
    amidst human frailty.
Our Supreme Being can even use
  those ever-present "weeds"
  to strengthen the seeds of goodness.
Often out of evil and death
  comes mysterious new growth,
  unexpected new forms of Life.
While humans cry for justice,
  divine time rolls on
  toward the inevitable harvest—
  when all weeds will be pulled,
    and good wheat harvested.

"The reign of God is like a mustard seed.
It is the smallest of the seeds,
  yet when full-grown,
  it is the largest of plants.
The birds of the sky come
  and build their nests in its branches" (Matthew 13:32).
God moves quietly yet surely.
Divine Power is as Water
  dripping incessantly upon rock,
    or as Fire
  slowly smoldering deep within.

What may seem small and ineffective
    becomes huge and powerful in the end.

Focus on the presence of "good seed"
    (God's unseen seeds of Truth and Life)
    instead of seeing the "bad weeds"
        all around you.
If at times you feel overwhelmed
    by the inexplicable presence
    of those "weeds"
        of inequity,
        injustice,
        and evil,
    call to mind the timeless wisdom
        of Paul's words.
"The Spirit helps us in our weakness . . .
    the Spirit makes intercession for us
        with groanings
    which cannot be expressed
        in speech" (Romans 8:26).

How Far Would You Go?

Seventeenth Sunday in Ordinary Time

(1 Kings 3:5–12; Romans 8:28–30; Matthew 13:44–52)

Walt Disney.
Few people achieve
what he did in life.
Creator of Mickey Mouse,
Donald Duck, and Snow White,
founder of Disneyworld,
producer of TV shows
and movies—
Disney was one of history's
truly gifted men.

Yet, did you know
he went bankrupt
several times?
Or that he had
a nervous breakdown
on his road to fame?
Disney succeeded because
he was willing to put *all* he had
into his dream.

He held back nothing,
   pouring every shred
      of his money,
         energy,
         self,
   into his unique vision.

Walt Disney had real commitment—
   not shallow words
      or surface actions,
   but total self-abandonment
      to his beliefs
      and dreams.
It is this level of commitment
   Jesus Christ speaks of
      in his parables.

"*The Kingdom of God is like
   a buried treasure which a man found;
   he sold all he had
      and bought the field*" (Matthew 13:44).
Possessing the Spirit of God,
   being transformed,
      healed,
         reborn in God's image
   is worth an entire fortune.
It is Something of inestimable value,
   totally beyond price
      or value,
   eternal in scope,
      endlessly replenished
      and replenishing.
Some would think a person crazy
   for digging up a field
      or
   selling one's belongings
   to possess such a Fortune.

But who would be the crazy one
    if someone found
    such a valuable Treasure!

How far would you go
    to possess the divine Treasure
        of God's Presence?
Once found, would you be willing
    to "sell all you have"
        to possess it?
Many people do indeed desire
    the Treasure of eternity
        with God,
    but are unwilling
    to "pay the price" of
        self-surrender
    to acquire it.

Possessing the infinite Treasure
    that is divine Love and Mercy
    means one's life can never
        ever
        be the same.
God demands all—
    and yet nothing—
    to purchase this Treasure.

"The Kingdom of God
    is like a merchant's search
        for fine pearls.
When he found a really valuable one,
    he put up for sale
    all he had and bought it" (Matthew 13:45).
Are you this deeply committed
    to searching for the Pearl
        of God's peace and power?

Is your spiritual commitment
    one of pious words
        and ritual actions,
    but lacking in passion
        and fiery intensity?
Has your faith journey
    become mired in worthless pearls
        of passing pleasures,
        empty promises,
        worldly obsessions?
Has your quest for the Divine
    become marked by
    skepticism and ritualism,
    caution and half-heartedness?
Even Jesus once said,
    "For many are invited,
        but few are chosen" (Matthew 22:14).

As you pray and take time for God,
    "ask God for whatever you want" (1 Kings 3:5).
But take Solomon's wisdom to heart.
Pray as he did
    for *"an understanding heart*
    to distinguish right from wrong" (1 Kings 3:9),
    to hold back nothing
        from your search
        for buried Treasure,
    to give your full measure
        for the greatest Pearl
        in the sea of Life.

Going to Jail

Eighteenth Sunday in Ordinary Time

(Isaiah 55:1–3; Romans 8:35–39; Matthew 14:13–21)

Recently I was in county jail.
I hadn't been sentenced,
    but had been invited
        to lead a Bible study.
People have strange ideas
    about jails and those jailed.
Many there likely had indeed
    done criminal things,
        deserving to serve time.
But what struck me immediately
    was the youthfulness of the faces
    and the startling Presence
        of God.

Jail is not a place one usually expects
    to find profound religious experience.
But that night with those prisoners,
    I saw men hungry and excited—
        for God and faith.
Those men thirsted for Truth
    and hungered for eternal Love.
"Jailhouse faith"? Perhaps.

But the lessons learned
   from being in jail
   could be learned by everyone.

"It is by grace that you have been saved
   through faith.
It is not your doing,
   neither is it a reward
   for anything you have accomplished—
     it is God's free gift" (Ephesians 2:8).
Those in jail could be condemned
   to many years in prison
     because of criminal actions.
But could not every one of us
   be sentenced and judged
     because of sinful actions?
Could not our own failures
   be justly held against us
     by our righteous God?
No one obtains heaven
   by their own actions alone.
Salvation is totally free—
   won only by Jesus' death
     on the cross,
   and your choice to accept it.

"All of you who are thirsty,
   come to the water!
Come without paying
   and without cost" (Isaiah 55:1).
All people should stand
   thirsting for waters of Mercy,
   humbled by sin before God,
   desperately in need of Divine Freedom.
All who are imprisoned by sin
   and locked up by fear
   can quench their thirst
     with the Waters of Life.

There is no price but humbleness,
   no cost but your pride.

"Who will separate us
   from the love of God?
Trial or distress,
   persecution or danger?" (Romans 8:35)
Your problems may not be as severe
   as those behind bars
      or awaiting sentencing.
But you, too, have severe challenges,
   personal problems and worries.
You, too, may at times feel
   that God is silent,
   that society has abandoned you,
   that your mistakes
      have cost you dearly.
Know today that nothing
   that comes from this world
      can do lasting harm.
Know that nothing made by humans
   can take from you
      the victory won by Jesus!

"In all these things
   we are more than conquerors
      through him who loved us" (Romans 8:37).
In all life-problems and fears,
   our God will not abandon us!
Our God even uses our struggles
   to transform our life-attitudes.
Thus, our burdens actually
   become blessings,
   and our imprisonments
      lead to freedom!

"Neither death nor life,
   angels or demons,
   present or the future,
   will be able to separate us
   from the love of God
      in Christ Jesus our Lord!" (Romans 8:39)
The love of our God is so great
   that God will walk with you
      at the darkest points,
      the most desolate places.
Not even the prisons of our problems
   deter our God from salvation.
Not even the jails of isolation,
   the cells of our loneliness,
      can keep God from us.
"Come to me heedfully,
   listen,
      that you may have life!" (Isaiah 55:3)

Be Not Afraid

Nineteenth Sunday in Ordinary Time

(1 Kings 19:9–13; Matthew 14:22–33)

A small boy was seated
  by himself in an airplane.
Noticing the boy's calmness
  on the long flight,
  a passenger asked,
    "Aren't you scared?"
The boy replied,
  "Nope.
  My daddy's the pilot!"

One of the most powerful forces
  in the world is fear.
Humans may deny and avoid it,
  but fear is the primal human emotion.
Some fear is instinctive:
  death, new job,
    loneliness,
    commitment.
Some results from personal woundings:
  relational problems,
  abandonment,
    hurts from the past.

One great misconception
   is that all fear is bad
      or useless.
But even the Bible speaks
      of healthy, constructive fear.
"The fear of the Lord
   is the beginning of wisdom" (Psalm 111:10).
The prophet Elijah hid in a cave
   as the glory of the Lord
      passed overhead.

The "fear of the Lord"
   is a naturally humbling response
   to a Power greater
      than our Self.
In all scriptural revelations
   of our Divine and Supreme Being,
   people had an awestruck fear:
   Isaiah, Jeremiah,
   Mary, Joseph,
      the apostles.
Humans should have healthy fear
   toward things in life
      that can harm them—
   threats to safety,
   impending danger,
      and
   the ultimate consequences
   of death (heaven or hell).
"Do not be afraid of those
   who kill the body . . .
   fear the One who has the power
   to cast into hell
      after you are dead!" (Luke 12:5)

The second side of fear, however,
   is negative and destructive.

Unnecessary fears can paralyze,
 holding us back
 from inner freedom
  and fullness of life.
This is what Jesus referred to—
 "Fear is useless.
 What is needed is trust" (Luke 8:50).

When facing the fears of life,
 your worries and stresses,
 or personal life-storms,
 keep the wisdom of the Master
  in mind.
Your God will come
 walking across water
  to save and soothe,
 speaking with calm Power:
 "Take courage! It is I!
  Be not afraid!" (Matthew 14:27)
God's Presence always pushes out fear—
 especially those unnecessary doubts,
 apprehensions, and worries
 lurking about
  in our inner dark places.

As you journey through this universe,
 wrestling with unseen forces
 that disturb and upset,
  learn to be at peace.
Sit quietly and calmly,
 resting your inner and outer Self
  in God's calming Presence.
Allow Peace to flow in you,
 through you,
  around you.
Take the last spoken words
 of the Master Jesus
 as your daily mantra:

"I am with you always
   until the end of time" (Matthew 28:20).
Learn from Peter's example:
   do not take your eyes
   from the Source
    of Peace and Power.
"Keep your eyes fixed on Jesus
   who inspires and perfects your faith" (Hebrews 12:2).

Have a healthy fear
   of the awesomeness
    of our great God.
Have no fear to walk forward
   through this world
   with your hand
   in the hand of the Man
    who stills the waters.

Spiritual Wealth Accumulation

Twentieth Sunday in Ordinary Time

(Isaiah 56:1–7; Matthew 15:21–28)

My father was a wise man
   who died much too soon.
Among the many lessons he taught me,
   he used to say,
"Try to put something away,
   and keep it for a rainy day."
Today, people pay financial advisors
   millions for the same advice:
   invest a little early and often,
   and watch it accumulate
      through the years.

This same financial wisdom
   applies in spiritual matters.
Your most valuable commodity
   is the Treasure of God
      within you,
   the powerful Seed of Faith
      growing inside.
"I have come to rate all as loss
   in light of the surpassing knowledge
      of the Lord Jesus" (Philippians 3:8).

Spirituality is life's greatest treasure—
    it, too, accumulates and accrues,
    is added to and amassed,
        over time.
It, too, can be exchanged,
    drawn upon,
    redeemed,
    put to very good use
        on Life's "rainy days."

But God forbid
    if your spiritual bank account
        is empty
    when the debts of despair
    and bills of problems
        start piling up!
Our gospel story today
    offers insight
        into spiritual wealth accumulation.
In all the Gospels,
    Jesus Christ praises but two people
        for their faith:
    a Roman centurion
        and this gentile woman.
Both were intensely persistent,
    deeply faith-filled.

This woman from Canaan
    (historic enemies of Jews)
    would not be deterred from the Treasure
        that was Jesus.
Despite being ignored,
    verbally rejected,
    she had an unshakable faith
        in both his Power
        and her humble need.

Aware that her own spiritual "wealth"
    couldn't cover the amount
        of her personal need,
    she humbly turned
        to Jesus Christ.

First, that woman had indeed
    the most valuable asset God looks for—
    utterly abiding
    and deeply humble faith
        in that Higher Power.
She could stand in weakness
    begging for freedom and healing
        from her God,
    because she already had
        a wealth of trust and hope.
"Faith is confident assurance
    about what we hope for" (Hebrews 11:1).

Second, this woman persisted
    in seeking her blessing.
She stubbornly refused to leave
    without obtaining the healing
        her daughter needed.
Jesus immediately recognized
    her great wealth of faithfulness.
"Woman you have great faith!
Your wish will come to pass" (Matthew 15:28).

Most of the time, spirituality
    is not about glorious faith experiences
        or explosions of insight.
Accumulating spiritual wealth
    is a matter of steady,
    unexciting, and even plodding
        persistence.

The Treasure of Faith
   is built slowly over time—
   by persistent prayer,
   faith-filled decisions,
     unselfish actions.
One wise man said,
   "Ninety percent of faith
     is simply showing up."

Do not grow impatient
   by the lack of progress
     or problems overwhelming you.
Your spiritual bank account
   is secure and ensured.
Just continue your daily deposits
   of prayer, trust, and charity.
Believe in future blessings
   despite present problems.
Stand up and say,
   "Although I am poor in spirit,
     I am wealthy in blessings!"

"If you have faith
   the size of a mustard seed,
     you can move mountains" (Matthew 17:20).
Build up your "seed-faith"
   into a great Treasure
     by persistent Love
     and undying Trust!
It will become
   your tree of Salvation
     in times of trouble.

Rocks of Refuge

Twenty-First Sunday in Ordinary Time

(Isaiah 22:15, 19–23; Romans 11:33–36; Matthew 16:13–20)

"On that day I will summon
my servant Eliakim . . .
I will fix him like a peg
in a sure spot" (Isaiah 22:20, 23).
While riding a ferry recently
    to a lovely Michigan island,
        I was struck by the many boats
            moored in the harbor.
All were held fast by anchors,
    with larger boats having two.
Securely moored by anchors,
    ships become safe
        in all but the worst of storms.

In the great sea that is Life,
    the ships of our souls
        have a similar need.

We need certain "anchors" in Life,
   definite foundation stones,
     unchanging "rocks"
to hold us secure
   when storms of the spirit
   or worldly worries arise.
Without fixed, unvarying anchoring points,
   humans flounder in uncertainty,
   struggling to make sense
     out of Life's nonsense.

What are the anchors,
   the "rocks of refuge,"
     in your life?

For most of us,
   certain people
     "anchor" our life.
Like Jesus today,
   we say to a select few,
   "I for my part declare to you,
     you are 'Rock' . . ." (Matthew 16:18).
Our close, intimate friends
   provide a secure foundation
     of love and acceptance
   in face of the challenges
     of Life's storms.

But any human anchor by definition
   is limited and fallible.
"Man is like a breath;
   his days, like a passing shadow" (Psalm 144:3).
All human spirits
   need reference points
     outside themselves.
This is why Jesus asked,
   "Who do you say that I am?" (Matthew 16:15)

This ultimate life-question
    immediately focuses
        all one's priorities.
It is an ageless question
    enduring through all centuries,
    echoing down to all people
        in all cultures.
Who is God to you?
What "holds you fast"
    as you journey through this world?
Indeed, our God is the eternal
    Anchor for all Life,
    the existential Horizon
        of our Universe,
    the ultimate Rock of Refuge.
"For from God and though God
    and for God all things are" (Romans 11:36).

But each human person has to make
    a personal choice for God
    as his or her own Anchor
        and Redeemer.
"You are the Messiah,
    the Son of the living God!" (Matthew 16:16)
From this conscious commitment
    to moor one's own spirit
        in God's Spirit,
    other "anchoring choices"
        logically flow:
        daily time spent in prayer,
        acts of justice done in Love,
        humble walking with God
            each day (see Micah 6:6).

Those who have anchored
    their spirits in God
    form a vast worldwide army
        best called "church."

Far surpassing mere ritual
    or religious formalism,
    the "true church"
        of God-trusting people
    is gifted with eternal Security,
        anchored in eternal Peace,
        fired by endless Passion.
"On this rock I will build my church,
    and the gates of hell
        will not overcome it" (Matthew 16:18).

Reflect today
    on the anchoring forces
        in your own life.
Is your life controlling you,
    or is God's Life empowering you?
Are you floating aimlessly,
    searching for Something
        to tie up to?
Rediscover the "Rocks"
    in your life.
Anchor your Self
    to the unchanging Power
        that is our God.

Fire in the Deep

Twenty-Second Sunday in Ordinary Time

(Jeremiah 20:7–9; Romans 12:1–2; Matthew 16:21–27)

Have you ever been tricked?
Has someone ever fooled you,
   perhaps deceived you
   in a way you resented?
It is one thing to be fooled
   as in a childhood game,
      but another
   to experience deception
      as an adult.
One feels betrayed,
   let down,
   disappointed—
and the result is often
   anger and resentment.

If you have ever felt this way,
   you can relate to Jeremiah.
Called by the Lord at an early age,
   God told him,

"Before you were born
  I dedicated you,
  a prophet to the nations
    I appointed you" (Jeremiah 1:5).
Despite uncertainty,
  Jeremiah never married,
  became a priest,
  worked hard,
  preached successfully
    in Israel.
Then in the middle of his life,
  a hostile king took the throne,
  precipitating a war.
Rebellion and ruin came
  to his homeland.

Jeremiah was angry,
  bitter, and resentful
    against the king and God.
"You tricked me, O Lord,
  and I let myself be tricked" (Jeremiah 20:7).
Feeling deceived,
  his work torn to shreds,
    his life now worthless,
  Jeremiah had every reason
    to abandon God and vocation.
"Every day I am an object of laughter,
  everyone mocks me" (Jeremiah 20:7).

There are times in life
  when we all feel this way—
  that our work is useless,
  the task ahead too daunting,
    the road too lonely.
In fact, it is guaranteed
  you *will* feel this way
    at some point
  on the road of Life.

When this happens,
   one's faith can be
      severely tested.
Some turn from God and religion
   in hollow disappointment.
"Yet another empty deception in life,"
some will say.

Yet, ironically, it is *then*
   that "deep faith" truly begins.
Moving past "nice God feelings"
   and easy "it-all-makes-sense faith,"
   the Fire in the Deep
      of God-wisdom
   can take over.
Jeremiah captures it well:
   "I say to myself,
      I will not mention him,
   I will speak his name no more.
   But then it becomes like fire
      burning in my heart,
      imprisoned in my bones.
   I grow weary holding it in" (Jeremiah 20:8–9).

God is not just a "nice feeling"
   one gets from prayer,
   but an uncontrollable Energy
      bursting forth.
God is that Power
   overwhelming any container,
   overflowing any "earthen vessel."
God is a fierce Fire
   gradually consuming everything,
   searing and transforming
      the landscape of our spirit.

When we are forced by life-events
   to face the deep, dark Wisdom
      of our mysterious God,
   our entire being will turn
      upside down.
Far from failing or falling,
   we come to a catalytic point
      in life and ministry.
The issue is *not* "being tricked";
   it becomes about that
      "Fire burning in my heart."
The issue is no longer human frustration,
   feelings of betrayal, weariness—
      it is about that unquenchable Fire
         raging
   in the deep places
      of our soul.

Learn to·move past external feelings
   of betrayal, anger,
      frustration, or tiredness.
Let go of your limited logic;
   let loose the uncontrollable Power
      that is God moving within.
Get in touch with the Fire
   of God's Spirit
      burning deep within.
"Do not conform yourself to this age,
   but be transformed
      by the renewal of your mind" (Romans 12:2).

Advance Warning

Twenty-Third Sunday in Ordinary Time

(Ezekiel 33:7–9; Matthew 18:15–20)

Warning labels.
They are everywhere:
  food packages,
  car interiors,
  airplanes,
  smoking containers,
  toy boxes,
  medicines.
"This product may have health risks."
"Do not use this while driving."

Thanks to modern advancements,
  we know much more today
  about the risks involved
  with various products and activities.
Groups and individuals feel it helpful
  (even obligatory)
  to warn others about
    possible danger
    or potential harm.

Prepared for what may happen,
    we live wiser,
    safer,
    healthier lives.

Our Creator-God
    has been in the "advance-warning business"
        for four thousand years.
As far back as Abraham,
    God warned his *anawim*
    (specially chosen people)
    about the dangers
    of not heeding his Wisdom.
Six hundred years before Christ,
    a man named Ezekiel
    received a unique mission:
        to be God's *"watchman"*
    in the world around him.
"You, son of man, I have appointed
    watchman for the house of Israel.
When you hear me say anything,
    you shall warn them for me" (Ezekiel 33:7).
This term had military connotations;
    a watchman was alert for danger,
    a sentinel against approaching enemies.

Being all-knowing and wise,
    God is the eternal Watchman
    when his people head astray.
Being beyond time and eternity,
    well aware of approaching dangers
        and Life's pitfalls,
    God's warnings are as valid today
        as they were generations ago.
Scripture is full of these
    "advance warnings" to God's chosen.

"Do not be conformed to this world,
    rather be transformed
        by the renewal of your mind" (Romans 12:2).
Because of God's immense love of us,
    God desires our transformation,
        both spiritual and personal.
Knowing this world can be
    both confusing and deceptive,
    God actively guides us
    along the path leading
        to heaven's gates.
Train your Self to listen well
    to the eternal Watchman's warnings.
Allow your Self to be "re-made"
    into the image and likeness of our God.

"If your brother should commit
    some wrong against you,
    go and point out his fault,
    but keep it between the two of you" (Matthew 18:15).
Giving legitimate, thoughtful,
    nonreactionary, loving warnings
        to others around you
    is essential in Life.
Although no one likes to warn people,
    or be accused of "meddling,"
    still, when we see sin or evil,
    it is our responsibility,
        out of love, to speak,
    and stand for Truth!
Learn well to become
    a gentle but persistent voice,
    a faith-full presence,
        for divine values
        and eternal Life.

"I have appointed you watchman . . .
when you hear me say anything,
you shall warn them for me."
The prophetic responsibility
for "en-fleshing" the Word of God
into human context
has passed to us.
The watchman's role comes down
from Ezekiel and prophets of old
to "new prophets"
in this generation.
Perhaps you are one—
the *anawim* chosen few
who will boldly witness to God,
be a voice for Truth,
a sentinel to salvation,
a watchman against evil and injustice.

Watch this world with eyes of Faith.
Fear not to warn of nearing dangers.
Witness to God's eternal Presence.
And do all these things
without righteous superiority,
but fired by Truth,
confident in Hope,
speaking always in Love.

Revolution!

Twenty-Fourth Sunday in Ordinary Time

(Sirach 27:30–28:7; Matthew 18:21–35)

"Should a person nourish enmity
against his fellows
and expect healing from the Lord?" (Sirach 28:4)
One hundred years ago,
 a holy man sought money
 to shelter neglected boys.
In approaching one group
 of hardened, nonbelieving men,
 one of them spit on him.
Calmly wiping his face,
 the man said,
"Thank you. That was for me.
Now what do you have for these boys?"

The most revolutionary teaching
 in all of world history
 is Jesus' teaching
  on forgiveness.
No other religion shares it
 with quite the same passion
  or radically deep import.

Islam believed in the "holy war"
    to spread their belief.
Judaism believed
    in "an eye for an eye."
Some Christian fundamentalists,
    even today, seem to prefer
    Yahweh's judgmentalism
        over
    Jesus' compassion.

But what the Master taught
    means radical surgery
        on our human attitudes.
"'How often must I forgive?'
Jesus replied,
    'Seventy times seven'" (Matthew 18:21–22).
To forgive when hurt,
    to act with compassion
        when resentfull—
these are both revolutionary
    and exceedingly difficult!

Apart from genuine abuse
    (sexual or physical or verbal)
    or serious social injustice,
    the wisdom of Jesus counsels
        letting go of grudges,
        releasing bitterness,
        moving past personal resentment.
Knowing that unforgiveness can kill,
    Jesus counsels the deep,
    and often difficult wisdom
        of mercy and compassion.

"Forgive your neighbor's injustice,
    then when you pray,
    your own sins will be forgiven" (Sirach 28:2).

Forgiveness is an attitude
    that begins early
        in one's faith journey,
    but truly takes a lifetime
        to learn well.
Forgiveness is never easy,
    certainly not always logical,
    but it can make perfect sense—
  if we understand
        what it is based upon.

Underlying this radical teaching
    is an even more radical concept:
    treat others
    the way your God
        has treated you!
"This is what love is—
    not that we have loved God,
    but that God has loved us" (1 John 4:4).

"Should you not have dealt mercifully
    with your fellow servant,
        as I dealt with you?" (Matthew 18:33)
The sizable debt of this gospel official
    was totally absolved by the king—
    a perfect paradigm
    for the countless sins of our soul
        and numerous personal failures
        forgiven by our God.

God's love for you is immense,
    undeserved, unending.
Has not his mercy and compassion
    for you been as well?
The revolution of Christian forgiveness
    demands one simple thing:
    that you give
        as you have received.

———

When can you stop forgiving?
When can people both
   "get mad and get even"?
When can humans rightfully hold grudges,
   nurture that bitterness
      that leads to genocide and war,
   or that blind ignorance
      that births racism and prejudice?

Only on one condition
   does the revolution of forgiveness
      ever end.
When God stops dying for you
   on the Cross.
When the One Creator of all
   stops blessing you
      with hope and peace.
When the Spirit of God
   stops empowering you
      and guiding you.
"This is my commandment,
   that you love one another,
   as I have loved you" (John 15:12).

The Curse of the Lottery

Twenty-Fifth Sunday in Ordinary Time

(Isaiah 55:6–9; Matthew 20:1–16)

*"Are you envious
    because I am generous?"* (Matthew 20:15)
Ann Landers once published
    the letter of a woman
    who won the lottery.
After great initial joy, the woman wrote,
    "Now I wish to heaven
    it had never happened."
Relatives she'd never heard of
    suddenly emerged.
Her mailbox couldn't hold
    the begging letters she got.
She said, "The thing that bothers me
    is that not one rejoices
        in my luck;
    in fact, they all have
        a sense of resentment.
Money changed my life for the worse."

Envy and jealousy
    are as old
        as the first human.

Among the seven deadly sins,
   they represent the dark side
     of the human condition.
Jealousy and envy proceed
   from perceived needs and wants.
They draw their dark energy
   from shallow values of
      possessing,
      comparing,
      acquiring.

In Matthew 20:2,
   workmen paid fairly
     "the usual day's wage"
   resented the owner's generosity
   in paying others the same amount.
The point of the story
   is the shallowness of measuring
     one's own Self
   by purely human standards
     of comparison.
Starkly contrasted here
   are God's gracious generosity
     and
   human pettiness and envy.

The Lord God gives freely
   to *all* people.
"The Lord is good to all . . .
   near to all who call on him" (Psalm 145:9).
How and what God chooses to do
   with any other person
     is not our concern.
Our own intrinsic value
   does not depend
     on what *other* people receive
     or are blessed with.

The value of a human person
   lies in his and her innate goodness,
   unique personal blessings,
    and giftedness.
All that is important for you
   is that your God knows you.
Your God knows what you need.
"My grace is enough for you" (2 Corinthians 12:9).

Take a good look today
   at your focus in life.
How do you look at life?
How do you make judgments
   about the reality around you?
Immature people
   focus on outer realities—
    other people,
    external things,
    possessions.
Mature people
   focus on inner realities—
    personal blessings,
    gifts given,
    the Spirit within.

Learn to "stay at home"—
   do not focus on
   what God is doing
    with your neighbor.
Worry, rather, about
   your own response to God,
   your own faithfulness
    to God's Presence
    and Mercy.
God's plan for all other people,
   indeed, the entire world,
    is not your concern.

"My thoughts are not your thoughts,
nor are my ways your ways,
says the Lord" (Isaiah 55:8).

Thank your Higher Power daily
for gracious generosity
and endless blessings.
Praise your Divine Creator this day
for what has been done,
is being done,
will be done,
in your own life.
Our God is an awesome God—
beyond measure, logic,
or human comprehension.
Give praise to the mysterious ways
of the God of all Ages!
"As far as the heavens
are above the earth,
so high are my ways
above your ways
and my thoughts
above your thoughts" (Isaiah 55:9).

Attitude Adjustment Hour

Twenty-Sixth Sunday in Ordinary Time

(Philippians 2:1–11)

"Your attitude must be Christ's" (Philippians 2:5).
During the "Michael Jordan years"
   of basketball greatness
      in Chicago,
   a commercial urged children
      to "be like Mike."

Every generation has its heroes:
   people who inspire others
   to copy their dress,
      style,
      actions.
Imitation is, indeed,
   the sincerest form
      of flattery.
However, for people seeking
   a deeper spiritual walk,
      there is no better role model
         for imitation
         than Jesus Christ.

"He did not deem equality with God
    as something to be grasped at" (Philippians 2:6).
The root flaw in the human psyche
    is ego and pride.
The sin of Adam in the Garden
    is humanity's sin—
        attempting to be God-like
            in ego-inflation
            or self-serving actions.

The life-attitude of Jesus
    reveals the road
    out of this singular self-obsession.
It is the road of breaking
        from God-like pretensions,
    of moving beyond the grasping urges
        and lustful needs
        of our darker side.
Even Jesus himself
    let go of his own divine status.
"Rather, he emptied himself,
    taking the form of a slave" (Philippians 2:7).

Jesus Christ is the great Hero,
    the only Person
        truly worth imitating.
This God-Man is the most balanced,
    most whole person
        who ever lived.
Totally comfortable with who he was,
    aware of his infinite value
        in the Father's eyes,
    the "Son of Man" thus had no need to
        defend,
        protect,
        promote,
        inflate his own ego.

Thus, Christ could "empty" himself
  for his stubborn people
    in selfless service
      and acts of Love.
"Each of you looking
  to others' interests
    rather than his own . . ." (Philippians 2:4).

This core "attitude adjustment"
  is at the very essence
    of our spiritual journey.
After being healed by tender Mercies,
  we are empowered by radical Grace
    to go out to others,
  beyond the limits
    of sin or Self.
Like our Master and Hero,
  we, too, will be "poured out"
  into this world as
    tools for justice,
      prophets of hope,
      sentinels to salvation.
"He humbled himself,
  obediently accepting even death" (Philippians 2:8).

The "attitude adjustment"
  that comes from following Jesus
    is a discovery of Truth.
Jesus knew Truth because he was Truth.
  Knowing his innate
    goodness and God-ness,
  he took on the task of
    incarnating that Truth and Love,
  accepting any and all consequences
    of his mission.

If you follow God fully,
    you, too, will know the Truth—
    the Truth of who you are,
        of whose you are,
        and who you work for.
And if you imitate your Master,
    convicted by the Name you act in,
    then you (like Jesus)
    should be prepared
        for any consequence.
In being like Jesus,
    there will be measureless blessings,
        but also unforeseen struggles.

Be like Jesus.
Live in his Power.
Walk through his Healing.
Catch the Fire of his Sprit.
Take hold of his total Freedom.
Know Jesus—and know Peace!
"At the name of Jesus,
    every knee must bend . . .
    every tongue proclaim
        JESUS CHRIST IS LORD!" (Philippians 2:11)

The Dark Side of Humanity

Twenty-Seventh Sunday in Ordinary Time

(Isaiah 5:1–7; Philippians 4:6–9; Matthew 21:33–43)

"They seized him, dragged him
outside the vineyard,
and killed him" (Matthew 21:39).
If the human race can be said
    to have a dark side,
    its propensity for violence
        must be it.

Despite humanity's amazing achievements
    in science, health, commerce,
    and information delivery systems,
    daily news reports
    still glaringly remind us of
    our primal proclivity
        for cruelty and violence.
Rape, murder, and robbery.
Physical abuse, domestic violence.
War, genocide, terrorism.
Gangs, drugs, "turf warfare."
Racism, prejudice, bigotry.

It seems the more civilized
   we become, the more insane
      our savagery becomes.

Even the Bible cannot escape
   the brutality humans are capable of.
The Prince of Peace himself,
   the One who healed the sick,
   raised the dead,
   brought hope to thousands,
      was a victim of violence.
"The light came into the world,
   but people loved darkness
      rather than light
   because their deeds were wicked" (John 3:19).
Matthew today speaks of men
   callous, cold, greedy,
   narrow-minded in their violence
      against the vineyard owner.
It is a story all too familiar
   to us today.

This propensity for violence
   is yet another effect
   of the original sin
      all humans are born with.
But thanks to our amazing Creator
   (who knows us better
      than we know ourselves),
   there is an exit
   out of the slippery slope of violence.
This "dark side" of humanity
   finds redemption in
      choosing Life
      and not death.
"Choose this day who you will serve" (Joshua 24:15).

The dark urges rising up in humans
 are transformed and healed
   only in the Life God gives,
   only by the Power available
  from a world beyond this one.
God alone moves our stubborn natures
 beyond human weakness,
   inherent sinful passions,
   dark energies,
  into new horizons of
   restoration,
   resolution,
   hope, and life.
"Live according to what
 you have heard me say
 and seen me do.
Then will the God of peace
 be with you" (Philippians 4:9).

Halting violence begins
 with your personal choices.
Make a personal life-commitment
 to help stop the violence
  rampant in society.
Choose to resist
 those dark human impulses
  that enslave
  and oppress so many.
Choose actions
 that promote Life,
 that arbitrate
  not alienate.

Teach your children well—
 that *"those who sow the wind*
  will reap the whirlwind" (Hosea 8:7).

Witness to the world
   by your own life-actions—
   that *"all those who draw the sword*
     will die by the sword" (Matthew 26:47).

Become an evangelist
   of Life and Truth,
   reminding all who will listen
   to *"seek first the Kingdom of God,*
     and all other things
     will be given you besides" (Matthew 6:33).
Guide others into the deep Wisdom that
   "thoughts should be directed
   towards all that is true,
   honest, pure, admirable,
     decent, virtuous,
     or worthy of praise" (Philippians 4:7).

Nothing Less than a Feast

Twenty-Eighth Sunday in Ordinary Time

(Isaiah 25:6–10; Philippians 4:12–20; Matthew 22:1–14)

In the long-ago eighteenth century,
   Austrian empress Maria-Theresa
   gave a fabulous wedding feast
      for her son Joseph II.
Aside from those invited to dine,
   three hundred others were invited *not* to eat
   but simply stand
      and watch the others eat!
And these three hundred considered it an honor
   to have been asked to be present!

Today, few in America would endure
   such foolish formality at a dinner.
Yet, many people do just that
   with their God:
   settling for less
   than God is willing to give.
Many settle for personal life-mediocrity
   when God's Life offers
   the fulfilling perfection
      of hope, health, and happiness.

Many settle for mere crumbs
    from the table of blessings,
      when the full loaf of divine Grace
        awaits them on the table.

Matthew tells it plainly today:
    we have been invited
      to eat with the Master!
"The reign of God is like a king
    who gave a wedding banquet
      for his son.
He dispatched his servants
    to summon the invited guests" (Matthew 22:2).
We are invited to a fabulous feast
    of food, fellowship,
      and faith
      with our Maker.
God's invitation is
    always open,
    always pending,
    always available.

In the Bible, the concept of
    invitation to a feast
    was a particularly powerful symbol.
For simple, agrarian Jewish people,
    being invited to share
    "juicy, rich food and
      pure, choice wine" (Isaiah 25:6)
    was a rare honor and privilege—
    one usually reserved
      for the wealthy and well off.
Jesus uses this image to speak to us
    not just of waiting blessings
      in this world,
    but the eternal Banquet
      awaiting us above,
    and the eternal Food

we need for nourishment
while on earth.
*"On this mountain
the Lord will provide
for all peoples
a feast of rich food
and choice wines"* (Isaiah 25:6).

The challenge for us on earth
is not whether God provides
for his beloved,
but rather how well we respond
to God's banquet blessings.
Matthew speaks of people
refusing to accept what God gives—
for selfish, stubborn, petty reasons.
"I'm too busy."
"I need to rest today—
Sunday is my only day off work."
"I have other more important things to do."
Sound familiar?
The king in Matthew's story
sent an army after such people—
symbolically saying that
God *demands* a response
when invitations are issued!

Examine your faith-life
and prayer-life today.
How much time do you spend
daily with your God?
Are you receiving
Food from heaven regularly—
partaking worthily of Eucharist,
the Bread of Life,
at your church?

Do you approach your God
   looking for a blessing
     or rather
   honoring out of duty?
Do you have an attitude
   of divine expectancy—
     "say only the word
       and I shall be healed" (Matthew 8:8)?
Are you a good steward of the gifts
   God *has* given you—
     using them fully and actively?

God has a feast of blessings
   and fulfillment awaiting you.
It will exceed your expectations,
   expand your mind and vision,
   soothe the hungers of your heart.
Your invitation has been issued.
Your response will be noted.
"My God in turn
will supply your needs fully,
   in a way worthy
   of his magnificent riches
     in Christ Jesus" (Philippians 4:19).

Attitudes of Gratitudes

Twenty-Ninth Sunday in Ordinary Time

(1 Thessalonians 1:1–5)

"*We keep thanking God*
  for all of you
  and we remember you
    in our prayers" (1 Thessalonians 1:2).
It is impossible to thank God enough.
No matter how frequent our prayer,
  how expressive our words,
  it is never enough to match
    what our God has done.

Thank you, God, for the world around us—
  for things great and small,
    beautiful and awesome,
  for splendor both seen and unseen.
Thank you for human life—
  for the infinite variety
  of colors, shapes, sizes;
  for our mutual hardships and hopes;
  for different ways of thinking
    and common patterns of dreaming.

"We are constantly mindful before our God
of the way you are proving your faith,
laboring in love,
showing constancy in hope" (1 Thessalonians 1:3).
Thank you, God, for grace in times of trouble—
for healing our diseases,
for Presence in the midst of pain,
for the courage of convictions
in a culture of confusion.
Thank you, God, for work to do—
for daily chores and gainful employment,
for the comradeship of shared labor,
for the challenges of living out Faith,
the Power of Love that renews,
the Energy of Hope that empowers,
the Fire of Passion that emboldens.

"We know too, beloved of God,
how you were chosen" (1 Thessalonians 1:4).
Thank you, God, for the blessings of my Self—
for calling, creating, choosing me
into this world,
for protecting me
from countless unknown dangers,
and not protecting me
when a challenge was needed.
Thank you, God, for salvation—
for the mystery of infinite Mercy,
for compassion in the face of compulsion,
for the forgiveness
that opened eternity for me.

Thank you, God, for relationships,
   for family and friends—
   for the mystery and joys
      of intimacy and love,
   for mutual forgiveness
      and shared burdens,
   for secrets kept in love
      and sorrows shared in silence.

"Our preaching of the gospel
   proved not a mere matter of words
      but one of power" (1 Thessalonians 1:5).
Thank you, God, for Power and miracles—
   for the mysterious ways our pains
      are transformed into gains,
   for the Life that springs up
      unexpectedly each and every day,
   for miracles of synchronicity
      and strange coincidence
      that never cease to amaze.
Thank you, God, for Mother Wisdom—
   those enlightening bursts
      of sudden insight,
      unexpected inspiration,
   that "dark Wisdom" of
      "my power made perfect
      in weakness" (2 Corinthians 12:9),
   the eternal Wisdom
      of your timeless Truth.

"It was carried on in the Holy Spirit,
*   out of complete conviction"* (1 Thessalonians 1:5).
Thank you, God, for growing up and growing old—
        for lessons learned,
        for rest in leisure,
        for insight deepened
            by experience,
        for time made precious
            by its passing.
Thank you for the Holy Spirit—
        for the energy, courage, boldness,
            of the "Paraclete,"
        for the gifts, peace, Presence,
            of the "Advocate,"
        for the One who prays in us,
            prompts our praise,
            and fires our deeps.
Thank you for Jesus Christ—
        who lived and died
            and lives again
            for our salvation;
        for our hope in him
            and the joy
            of serving him.
Amen.
    Amen!
        Amen!

Love Is Not a Feeling

Thirtieth Sunday in Ordinary Time

(Exodus 22:20–26; Matthew 22:34–40)

The huge eighteen-wheel semi
   pulled up to a truck stop.
As fellow truckers watched
   from nearby diner windows,
   a middle-aged man emerged,
   removing a wheelchair
    from the back cab.
Opening the passenger-side door,
   the burly trucker put his arms
   around a woman, physically lifting her
    out and into the chair.
After arranging her carefully,
   closing the truck door,
   he pushed her into the diner.
From a now silent table of truckers
   came the quiet comment,
    "Now that is love."

Indeed it is.
No word is more misused,
　　more misunderstood
　　in our English language
　　　　than *love.*
The ancient Latin language
　　actually had four words for it,
　　but our single English word
　　is misused for everything—
　　from wheels to meals,
　　from delightful toys
　　　　to ecstatic joys.
And when it comes to relationships,
　　commitment, or spirituality,
　　people easily toss around the word *love*
　　with little clue
　　　　as to the transformational Truth
　　it represents.

"Which commandment of the law
　　is the greatest?" (Matthew 22:36)
Why love, of course—
　　but not merely the love
　　of momentary ecstasy,
　　instinctual fulfillment,
　　　　passing pleasure.
Love is not a feeling.
True love is a decision—
　　a time-tested commitment
　　involving every level
　　　　of a person's being.
True love may begin as a passionate fire,
　　but it endures only if the fuel
　　of one's total being
　　　　is consumed to keep it burning.

"You shall love the Lord your God
   with your whole heart,
   whole soul, whole mind.
This is the greatest commandment" (Matthew 22:37).
Perhaps people do not know
   how to love others
   because they do not
   love their God
      first and foremost.
The transformational power of Love
   is best experienced,
   and only truly understood,
      in a prioritized life.
Frenetically "grabbing" love
   wherever it may be found
      inevitably ends in frustration.

Is your life "ordered" around God
   in the first place,
   the central place,
      the core place,
   of all activities and dreams?
The wisdom of thousands of years
   and countless humans cries out
      to this modern world:
"Seek first the Kingdom of God,
   and all these other things
      will be given besides" (Matthew 6:33).

"The second is like it:
   'You shall love your neighbor
      as yourself'" (Matthew 22:39).
Actually there are two commandments here.
The true "second commandment"
   is love your Self.
A person honors, respects, values others,
   only as they honor, value, and respect
      their Self first.

You are, indeed, a priceless treasure
    in this vast universe.
You are *"God's work of art"* (Ephesians 2:10),
    unique in gifts and beauty.

But loving Self
    is not ego-inflation
    or pompous pride.
"Loving Self" is a decision—
    submitting to healthy life-discipline,
    honoring one's body
        by wise life-choices,
    respecting the eternal Spirit within.

"Do to others
    as you would have them do to you" (Luke 6:31).
The final divine injunction
    follows logically from these—
    respect and honor all
        who cross your life-path.
"Loving your neighbor" is
    compassion, kindness, respect,
        at all times—
    but courage, forgiveness, "tough love,"
    at challenging times.
Always live your life
    so that someone from afar
    might say of you,
        "Now that is Love."

"Pretending" Games

Thirty-First Sunday in Ordinary Time

(Matthew 23:1–12)

Who has not pretended in life?
Pretended to be someone else—
 an athlete, a movie star,
  some special person?
Pretended to be somewhere else—
 on a desert island,
 in a fantasy world,
  a "getaway" place?

"Pretending games" are normal,
 a healthy part of early development—
 but when carried later into life,
 they take on a different character.
If indulged in wisely and judiciously,
 "pretending" can still relax,
 even rejuvenate
  the stressed-out adult psyche.

But adult "pretending" games
 can become sources of stress
 and signs of a psyche
  out of harmony with Self.

The different masks people assume
   in various areas of adult life
   can be disruptive
      of inner peace and balance.
It requires great insight, integrity,
   and personal honesty
      to keep one's life-balance.

But perhaps the worst games
   people play are with God.
The Bible has a simple word
   for such "pretending" games:
      hypocrisy.
Hypocrisy is when one's
   external words and actions
   do not match up with
      internal truths and Reality.
"Their words are bold,
   their deeds are few.
They bind up loads heavy to carry,
   while they themselves
   will not lift a finger
      to budge them" (Matthew 23:4).

In one's personal spiritual journey,
   the lack of consistency,
      commitment,
      or integrity
   with the Supreme Being
      is a serious issue.
Our God is all about basic honesty,
   personal integrity,
      humbleness of heart.
Our God is not about saying one thing
   and doing another.

The spiritual journey is not about
   pretense or falsehood,
     but rather about
   personal life-change,
   transformation in Love,
     attitudes of integrity.
The very essence of Divinity
   is Truth-full integrity and consistency—
   outer actions
     matching inner attitudes,
   outer faith
     reflecting inner faith.

"Whoever humbles themselves
   will be exalted" (Matthew 23:12).
The antidote for "games" of hypocrisy
   is humbleness of heart.
Humility is the most denigrated,
   ignored, forgotten virtue
     of this modern age.
People today seem to prefer
   living in the darkness of pretense,
   playing games, covering up,
     rather than
   walking in the Light
     of Truth and Integrity.

Humility is simply truth—
   standing naked before Divine Truth,
     and then
   living and acting
     in basic human truth.
Humility is facing the truth
   that we are both blessed and broken,
   both full of Grace
     and yet in need of Mercy.

Humility is truth
   about the "games people play"
     to find elusive peace.
"The Lord takes delight in his people,
   God crowns the humble with salvation" (Psalm 149:6).

The truth is that you are precious,
   beloved, and unique in this universe.
The truth is that human actions
   are frequently selfish and self-serving.
The truth is that God is
   far more patient with us
     than we are with each other.
The truth is that we need to
   sit silently before our God,
   drinking in some simple Truths:
     I am.
     God is.
     That is enough.

Be still this day.
Move past life's falsehoods
   into eternal Truth.
Be still and know
   that God is enough.
Be still and become aware
   of your "pretending" games.
Be still and know.
   Be still.
     Be.

Wedding Wisdom

Thirty-Second Sunday in Ordinary Time

(Matthew 25:1–13)

"The Kingdom is like ten bridesmaids
who went out to welcome the groom" (Matthew 25:1).
Throughout history,
few events have generated
more excitement than weddings.
Marriage customs and rituals
vary much from culture to culture—
from arranged unions, eloping,
and formal engagements,
to "jumping the broom,"
smashing glasses,
and wearing crowns.

Weddings are events
of powerful symbolism.
They represent the continuation
of one's lineage,
the perpetuation of family
through children.
They express and fulfill
that deep human longing
for love and intimacy.

They contain elements
    of family reunion (and tension!),
    the formality of ritual and tradition,
    the celebratory eating
        connected with great banquets.

Jesus Christ often used
    Jewish wedding customs
        to teach key life-wisdoms.
In ancient Israel
    it was the public engagement ceremony
        that bound two people together.
Then the groom prepared the house,
    eventually coming in procession
    with his friends for the wedding
        to claim his bride.
This procession led to a celebration,
    often at night,
        often delayed by preparations.
A great banquet ended the festivities—
    a rare treat for mostly simple,
        agricultural people.
"Blessed are those
    who are invited
    to the wedding supper of the Lamb!" (Revelation 19:9)

Jesus used the wedding banquet
    as a symbol of the fulfillment
    and eternal joy of heaven.
The goal of human Life is
    eating at the eternal Banquet,
    being judged worthy to sit
    at the King's own table.
"Happy is the person
    who eats bread
    in the Kingdom of God" (Luke 14:15).

Breaking bread with the Lord in heaven
   should be the single-minded goal
   of all your actions,
      dreams,
      prayers.
Whatever you do,
   whatever life-choices you make,
   whoever you make them with—
   let them push you,
      guide you,
      lead you,
   beyond this world's limitations
      to the next world's eternity.
"I am the living bread.
   If anyone eats this bread,
      they shall live forever" (John 6:51).

But some of the bridesmaids
   failed the *one* job they had:
   to be alert and prepared
   to greet the groom
      and enter this banquet.
"The foolish ones,
   in taking their torches,
      brought no oil along" (Matthew 25:3).
Their mistake was twofold:
   in sleeping they were unaware
      of the groom's coming,
   and they had neglected specific behaviors
      key to entering the wedding.

Although today their mistake seems slight,
   its symbolic ramifications were profound.
"The ones who were ready
   went into the banquet.
Then the door was barred.
'Master, master,' they cried,
   'Open the door for us!'

But he answered, 'I tell you,
    I do not know you'" (Matthew 25:11–12).

This "wedding wisdom" of Jesus
   is as important for us today
      as it was then.
Be alert for the Groom's coming
   at whatever time,
      in whatever form!
God has a history of showing up
   unexpectedly
      to surprise people!
It takes great vigilance,
   constant alertness,
   deep sensitivity to the Spirit,
      to sense God's silent Presence in Life.
"Keep your lamps burning brightly . . .
   be on guard!" (Luke 12:35–40)

Your ticket to heaven's eternal Banquet
   is free—but has a price.
The price of admission is
   alertness to divine Presence;
   actions and words
      of justice and kindness;
   faithfulness in prayer and worship.
"Keep your eyes open,
   for you know not the day or the hour" (Matthew 25:13).

Gifted and Accountable

Thirty-Third Sunday in Ordinary Time

(1 Thessalonians 5:1–6; Matthew 25:14–30)

"[A man] called in his servants
and handed his funds over to them
according to each one's abilities" (Matthew 25:14).

Two men—two stories.
Tom was a bright, promising youth—
   a talented young student and athlete.
Ten years later,
   his gifts unrealized,
   his marriage a shambles,
   he was arrested and jailed
     for selling drugs.
His bright future had vanished.
Today, no one knows him.

Harlan was a young man
   born in Kentucky
   to poor parents.

Being the eldest child
  of a very large family,
   he had to do all the cooking
    for his younger siblings
    while his parents worked.
Harlan accepted this responsibility,
  dedicating his youthful energy
   to caring for his family
    in whatever way he could be of support.
Gradually, Harlan became quite skilled
  in his unique style of cooking.
Today, his cooking is famous,
  and his name a legend:
    Colonel Harlan Sanders,
    Kentucky Fried Chicken.

Two gifted men, and yet
  two very contrasting life-stories.
Both were amazingly gifted—
  yet one's gifts were never realized,
  and the other's changed the world.
Tom *"went off, dug a hole in the ground"* (Matthew 25:18)
  with his gifts.
Harlan was *"an industrious and reliable servant,*
  put in charge of larger affairs" (Matthew 25:23).

The contrast of these two
  gives us a context to reflect
   upon our own God-giftedness.
The Creator-God designed you
  with astounding gifts and talents.
You were endowed with amazing faculties
  of memory and dexterity,
  of physical proficiency,
   psychological capacity,
   mental agility,
   verbal fluency.

*"You have made us
  a little less than the angels,
  and crowned us
    with glory and honor"* (Psalm 8:6).

God's legacy to you upon entering this existence
  was that unique blend of
    thought, appearance,
    skills, and wisdom
    that makes you YOU!
All of these gifts are knit together,
  weaving a beautifully interwoven mosaic
    that is your truest Self.

We walk this world for but a short time—
  but we have been placed here
  with all we need
    (and more!)
  to make a success of our Self.
*"You are God's handiwork,
  created in Jesus Christ
  to lead a life of good deeds
  which God prepared for you
    in advance"* (Ephesians 2:10).

But your amazing gifts come
  with a price tag.
God gives freely,
  but divine gifts are never fulfilled
    without some graced response in return.
The price tag for your beauty and skills
  is personal accountability
    for what you have been given.
*"When much has been given a person,
  much will be required"* (Luke 12:47).

What are you doing
  with your unique God-giftedness?

———

How have your gifts
    made a difference in this world?
How have they made a difference
    in *one* person's life?
How have your gifts multiplied,
    been increased through use,
    education,
    life-challenges?
Are your varied skills being well used—
    mental and physical agility,
    psychological and interpersonal adeptness,
    specific "hands-on" applied skills,
        abstract reasoning logic?

Beware the trap
    of "routinizing" your talents.
Constantly push your Self to grow,
    to increase your God-gifts
        through use and education.

Beware the trap
    of comparing your Self
        with others.
Your gifts are *your* gifts.
There is no one like you—
    and no one will be held accountable
    for your life and actions
        but *you.*

Never underestimate your Self
    or your God.
Your human potential is infinite,
    just as your spiritual Power
        in God is endless.
You are *"a child of the light and of day.*
    Therefore let us not
    be asleep like the rest,
        but awake and sober!" (1 Thessalonians 5:6)

Don't Sweat the Small Stuff?

Christ the King

(Ezekiel 34:11–17; Matthew 25:31–46)

It is a popular phrase:
    "Don't sweat the small stuff."
Don't worry about the small things,
    the unimportant minutiae
        that bother us in life.
Keep the big picture,
    stay mellow and cool.

This is not a bad philosophy of life,
    as far as it goes—
        but it *only* goes so far.

In January of 1986,
    I wonder if mechanics
    on the *Challenger* space shuttle
    said, "Don't sweat it"
    upon seeing a worn, minuscule part
        called an "O ring."
If so, seven people died
    when it launched that day.

People do not want airline mechanics
    saying, "Don't sweat the small stuff"
    as they perform
        last-minute pre-flight checks.
People don't buy a new house
    with a hairline crack
    in the foundation and say,
        "Don't sweat it—it's small."

There are some things in life
    which require and demand
    that attention be paid
        to "little things"—
    for on these very things
    one's entire life and future
        may depend.

Perhaps this was on Jesus' mind
    shortly before he died,
    as he told people
        what heaven would be like.
"When the Son of Man comes in glory,
    he will sit on his royal throne,
    and all the nations
        will be assembled before him" (Matthew 25:31–32).

Now that advance warning itself
    should have made people
        sit up and listen.
But Jesus' description
    of the "dress code"
        for entry into eternal glory
    should be indelibly etched
        on every mind.

It is *not* the major life-achievements
    humans rejoice in,
  not the marks of honor
    the world bestows,
  not even the things
    we are often most proud of—
  job, children, success,
  prosperity, religion.
It seems entering heaven depends upon
  the very "small stuff"
    some say not to "sweat about"!
"I was hungry and you gave me food . . .
  thirsty and you gave me drink . . .
  a stranger and you welcomed me,
    naked and you clothed me . . .
  ill and you comforted me,
    in prison and you came to visit me"
  (Matthew 25:35–36).

This may come as a shock to some—
  self-important power brokers,
  the "rich and famous,"
    self-righteous religious,
    and others.
But entry into heaven
  is utterly dependent
    on "small things"
    done in love
  to people around us.
After all the books are written,
  all the speeches given
  expounding on
    what is important in life—
  the bottom line
    is attitude and action.

Attitude! "Did you see me
    in the people around you?"
Is your vision of life big enough,
    open enough, to see God
      when others are blind?
Did you live your life
    focused on the greatest priorities?
*"Seek first the Kingdom of God,
    and all this will be given you besides"* (Matthew 6:33).

Action! "Did you act in love
    when I appeared in your life?"
Did you reach beyond
    your busy lifestyle
      and self-important priorities
    to give to others
    what they could not get
      for themselves?
Did you leave your self-absorbed world
    to perform simple, basic acts of love
    to the broken and burdened
      around you?
Did you live life lovingly
    twenty-four hours a day?

*"I assure you,
    as often as you did this
    for one of the least,
      you did it for me"* (Matthew 25:40).
And even more importantly—
    *"As often as you neglected to do it
    to one of these little ones,
      you neglected to do it to me"* (Matthew 25:45).